DEATH TALK

Conversations with Children and Families

Glenda Fredman

Foreword by
Tom Andersen

Systemic Thinking and Practice Series

Series Editors
David Campbell & Ros Draper

Routledge
Taylor & Francis Group

LONDON AND NEW YORK

First published 1997 by Karnac Books Ltd.

Published 2018 by Routledge
2 Park Square, Milton Park, Abingdon, Oxon OX14 4RN
711 Third Avenue, New York, NY 10017, USA

Routledge is an imprint of the Taylor & Francis Group, an informa business

British Library Cataloguing in Publication Data

A C.I.P. record for this book is available from the British Library.

ISBN 9781855751743 (pbk)

Edited, designed, and produced by Communication Crafts

DEATH TALK

For
Ralph Gus Fredman and Emmah Mazwi Gumede

ACKNOWLEDGEMENTS

Although I take sole responsibility for the written words in this book, I cannot take full credit for the ideas and the thinking that informs them, since these have been developed and formed in conversations with many people with whom I have had the privilege to enter into relationship.

I am indebted to the children, families, colleagues, and course participants with whom I created the material for this book.

Sue Krasner joined me in convening training workshops on children and death, and I continue to value the opportunities we made together to elaborate our own stories about death and dying.

Adam Phillips's supervision balanced clarity with the unusual, helping me to go on in my work with new meanings and enthusiasm; his warmth and compassion allowed me to sit with not-knowing and to take time finding words to fit the intensity of my experiencing; his multifaceted encouragements inspired me to write this book.

The opportunities to work and talk with Peter Lang have extended my thinking; through his generosity, creativity, and language, I have found grammars to reflect within this book many of my practices.

Joe Cavanagh helped me endure and overcome several computing crises during the preparation of the manuscript; without his patience and support the print would never have reached the page.

From Sheila Fredman, my mother, I have learnt the "art" of creating stories; I continue to marvel at her natural talent for appreciative re-authoring.

I would never have written this book without the loving contributions of Philip Messent. His constant validation and enthusiasm for the project, his remarkable willingness to listen to my incessant musings about its content and form, and his discerning comments on each chapter and revisions made the process of writing this book an absolute pleasure for me.

CONTENTS

EDITORS' FOREWORD

When our series was conceived years ago, we were inspired by the power of systemic thinking and the possibility of putting these ideas into practice in a range of different settings. *Death Talk* is exactly the kind of book we had in mind. It distils very sophisticated clinical work into a simple language and simple technique for talking to children, making it accessible to a much wider range of practitioners than trained psychotherapists and family therapists. The book is about the healing power of conversation. It gives numerous examples of children and their families being released from the grip of sadness, isolation, and fear by talking about their own experiences of death. Not only does the author, Glenda Fredman, tackle head-on the great taboo subject, but she embues the reader with the conviction that an open, respectful conversation about death will, in itself, bring about therapeutic change.

The theoretical framework of the book is based on the contemporary ideas of narrative therapy, and the author illustrates her work, free of theoretical jargon, with many examples of helping children to construct new stories about their experiences. The book is not about aligning her approach with one model of child development. In fact, she acknowledges the validity of many models, as she goes on her way to explore the real subject of the book: talking to children. The book is written in a straightforward style that makes it seem as though Fredman is just having a chat with a child. The power of her approach is not immediately evident, but it is a continuous, gentle offering of space for children to bring their feelings, to hear themselves talking, and to hear the therapist validating their experiences. The style is also one that lends the reader readily to say, "Oh, I can do that".

There is a growing interest in the field for work with children, as if they have been overlooked in some of the enthusiasm to talk "systems talk", and this book makes a great contribution to shifting the focus to the child, while at the same time giving numerous examples of work with parents and whole families and documenting examples of how parents were helped indirectly through the work with the child. The book should prove invaluable for many practitioners, such as teachers, nurses, doctors, and counsellors who have everyday contact with children, as well as the therapists who work with children in hospital and clinical settings. The way of thinking and the skills presented here are fundamental to systemic practice, and they will provide a platform for many clinical interviews besides those with children talking about death.

David Campbell
Ros Draper
London
October 1997

FOREWORD

Tom Andersen

This is a beautiful book, a book with a lot of sweet and strong touches; it moves. And it is very ready for the reader. Since the book speaks so well for itself, I have deliberately kept this foreword short. Maybe you, the reader, should leap over this and read the book first, and then eventually come back to my words.

When the author, Glenda Fredman, asked me to write the fore-word, I thought that my present overload of work had to result in: "I feel honoured to be asked, but . . ." The decision *not* to write had actually been made when the manuscript arrived, but, reading the first page, my mind started to change, and in the middle of page two I thought: I *will* write!

It is always an honour to write a foreword—and a serious task, since authors always put so much of their selves into a book. As I met Glenda only for a brief lunch-talk in relation to a workshop that I gave in London in November 1996, I cannot, unfortunately, write about her. I would have liked to, because meeting her in her own book stirs so many good thoughts and feelings.

This book is in ordinary, daily language—in itself, a great relief. It presents the various situations first, then come the after-thoughts on a more philosophical level. It moves between these levels all the time.

It is not only a book for those who are open to learn and enlarge their repertoire, but it also suggests how to learn and teach, both oneself and others. It offers an abundance of good ideas for difficult practical situations: for instance, what to ask or what to do.

The book strongly emphasizes that we reach a position of "Now I know how to go on" (Wittgenstein) through talking with each other. It moves us away from what we so easily do—namely, saying to ourselves, "What shall I do?"—to saying in the open, "What do we do?"

The book says that there is not one right way to live just as there is not one right way to die, that one should never take anything for granted. We have to ask, for instance, is this the time to talk or is it a time for silence?

The book marvels wisdom, and the reader might be reminded of Ecclesiastes: "For everything there is a season, and a time for every matter under heaven; a time to be born and a time to die; a time to plant and a time to pluck up what is planted; a time to kill and time to heal; a time to break down and a time to build up; a time to weep and a time to laugh; a time to mourn and a time to dance; a time to cast away stones and a time to gather stones together; a time to embrace and a time to refrain from embrace; a time to seek and a time to lose; a time to keep and a time to cast away; a time to rend and a time to sew; a time to keep silence and a time to speak; a time to love and a time to hate; a time for war and a time for peace." This book by Glenda moves the reader gently through various kinds of time.

The book made me happy, even if the issues are very sad and very serious: the issues of death and dying, the issues of leaving and being left. I found myself in many places as I read the book. At first high up in the mountains, where I could see the Arctic Ocean out there. At first it was quiet, and the sun poured down on snow-covered mountains. Then I started to hear singing voices, first one, then more and more appeared, until I was surrounded by a full choir and actually took part in it. And the singing brought all the feelings:

the sad ones, the fearful ones, the angry ones, the happy ones. All of them.

What of Glenda, the author? I highly appreciate her taking such a strong "non-expert" stance. She is very respectful towards ordinary, daily language and traditions. She very much represents the post-modern reaction towards modern time.

The Finnish professor in philosophy Georg Henrik von Wright writes about the shifts from medieval time (500 to 1500) to modern time (1500 to 1950) to postmodern time (after 1950). He says that the "big" words in medieval time were *authoritarian doctrines*. These were set by the church and the kings. The other big word was *obedience*: the people should obey the doctrines. Modern time came as a reaction to this, and the new big words became: *liberty, rationality, independence*. People should govern their own lives from inside themselves, and they should be individually responsible for their successes and failures. Other big words—*natural sciences, techniques, market economy, progress*—became a very powerful combination for people to enrich their lives. However, von Wright says, people of the modern time have gone too far in their greediness for progress and sweet life—so far, that we are now critically drowning in problems: the threat of a nuclear disaster, millions of people starving to death, the global imbalance of temperature as a result of pollution, and so forth. These enormous problems von Wright understands as consequences of *not* putting our activities in the perspectives of ethics and aesthetics. These perspectives belong to traditions and are carried by ordinary, daily language. How have we come to forget these perspectives? Most probably because our language bewitched us into forgetting. The language of progress and technicalities and rationality and economy is a language of expertise—the language of the expert—and is foreign to ordinary life. The postmodern period represents a reaction to the modern period. We must try to rewind, to bring back traditions, to bring back ordinary, daily language. This book and its author are welcome participants in this movement.

Glenda also said, when she asked me to write the Foreword: "If only I had attended your workshop before I had written this book, I most certainly would have approached it differently."

I wonder what would be different? Maybe she would have included something about outer and inner voices? Maybe she would have let the reader hear her inner voices? Let the reader know how she speaks with herself in all the sensitive moments she is going through?

If she had, might we not only hear her but see her more? How she tilts her head slightly and looks in the other's face of pain such that the other feels comforted? Or how she carefully lets her one hand take care of her other hand in moments of silence and stillness when she does not want to disturb? I must confess I would have liked to see that.

The book is so gentle, as if to say: "Be with me! I shall take good care of you!" And it does.

Setting the scene

The ideas for this book emerged while I was working as a Clinical Psychologist with children and families on a paediatric ward of a large general hospital in London. The people using this hospital represented the population of London—multiethnic, multicultural, multilingual, reflecting a richness of race, culture, and religion. My responsibilities included support and therapy with staff and families where a child was diagnosed with a terminal illness, was dying, or had recently died. I was also working with children who had lost a parent or sibling.

The first child I was asked to see was a Russian girl aged 10 and her mother. The child had a form of leukaemia with a poor prognosis. Neither child nor mother spoke any English, and I speak no Russian. The girl, I was told, was hysterical every time she received intravenous chemotherapy. I was ushered by the nursing sister into the isolation room to find an emaciated girl, sallow to the extent that she looked an orange-tinted shade of beige. She was howling and shaking, and her mother sat in the diagonally opposite corner, rocking and groaning. I searched for the theory to apply to this situation—I could find nothing that fitted the extent of their suffering, the girl's age, or the differences between their language and culture and my own.

At the time of starting this job I was using a range of psychological theories and techniques to guide my approach to bereavement, loss, and mourning. These included the practices and theories of Freud (1917), Bowlby (1969, 1973, 1980, 1989), and developmental psychology (Kane, 1979; Piaget, 1958), the teachings of Elizabeth Kubler-Ross (1970, 1983) and Colin Parkes (1972), and the methods of behavioural and psychodynamic psychology. I believed in the importance of talking about death and dying with bereaved people and the necessity for the bereaved or families of the dying to talk about the death with each other.

As I continued to involve myself in conversations with children and families, however, I noticed that clients may prefer to talk with friends rather than with professionals and learnt that not talking about death more often reflects inappropriate contexts of time, place, or relationship than an inability to talk about death. I therefore began to explore different possible meanings of death talk. Chapter One shows how families and professionals challenged my views that death talk is necessarily the domain of experts and requires specialist training and professional experience and that death talk is essential to ensure a good dying outcome. I go on to discuss how we can simultaneously hold a range of beliefs about death talk, which we draw from our personal and professional contexts such as those of family, culture, gender, religion, and training, and I report what people say to me, to illustrate how beliefs about death might sit comfortably together or contradict each other, creating conflict or confusion within or between individuals. I show how professionals sometimes elevate professional theories over personal views to reconcile these sorts of dilemmas. Instead of construing our beliefs as obstacles to be overcome, I propose that all beliefs about death talk could be used as resources to inform conversations between helpers and clients when "talking about talking" about death.

In Chapter Two I address how to set a context for talking about death and dying which takes into account whether and when to talk as well as the relationships and identities of the child, the family, and those significantly involved. Initially joining with the child and network of carers in conversations to establish the "context of knowing and telling", I explore what each significant person knows about the child's health status, their recognition of each other's awarenesses, and the beliefs that they all hold about people knowing and telling. I suggest asking questions about what the child knows and what the child's carers think he or she should know, instead of presuming the child's understanding on the basis of a psychological model of child development that assumes a standard developmental process and ignores the relevance of culture, religion, race, class, and gender, as well as the uniqueness of the dying child's experience. Rather than locating the knowledge in the child, therefore, I explore how the child constructs his or her knowledge in relationship with family, culture, community, hospital, and other significant contexts. Becoming more curious about the different theses that people hold about children's knowledge and understandings, I attempt to invite the family and carers to become observers to their own beliefs, feelings, and relationships and to share such observations in our creating together a "context of knowing and telling".

This book is written from the perspective of one who is not an expert on bereavement, with the view that it is not possible to become an expert on the death or dying of others. Many books on the subject start from the premise that it is possible to die or grieve in a right or a wrong way, and they go on to give advice to this end. In Chapter Three, I suggest that the few psychological death theories of experts in the field have been ritualized and turned into policy and procedures for good practice on how to die and how to deal with death and dying in order to manage the pain and anxieties associated with death. In some circumstances commitment to such theories and policy has dominated helpers' relationships with clients. Examples of what clients actually say to me are presented to illustrate situations in which premises and practices conventionally used in bereavement work neither meet their needs nor reflect their experience and how in some circumstances they experience such approaches as undermining or an affront. In this way I challenge the universal application of "stage" theories of grieving and the assumption that a successful resolution to mourning requires saying goodbye to the deceased. For example, instead of construing "denial" as a state outside the client's conscious intention, my conversations with "denying" clients show how they have a degree of awareness of which professionals are not conscious, and how they control how much they want to know or not know in relation to contexts of time, place, or who is available to support them.

I therefore move away from the notion of emotions as descriptions of self, inner states, or ways of being which should be attributed by adults to children, or by professionals to clients. Instead I construe emotions as the theories that we construct in communication with people with whom we are in relationship. Our decision to choose one (emotion) theory over another will be influenced by the extent and quality of meaning that the construction gives to our experience, the effects it has on ourselves and our relationships, and its use towards helping us know how to go on. Examples in Chapter Three of my conversations with clients illustrate how acknowledging the child's and the family's expertise on their own feelings contributes to the construction of a meaningful and useful language and theory of emotions, thereby facilitating a context for the child and significant others to go on.

Over time I began to notice that I was having a limited range of conversations about death, dying, bereavement, and mourning with those facing the death or dying of close family members. Despite the rich variation among the children and families with whom I was talking, I recognized that I was returning to the same restricted repertoire of theories to inform my thinking and hence what I said. Therefore I often found that the ideas I was using did not fit with the needs or experience of my clients—for example, the age of the dying patient or mourning family member, their stage of life or death, or their religious or cultural beliefs.

At around this time I was introduced to the narrative approach (White & Epston, 1990), which describes how we organize and make sense of our experience in terms of stories or narratives. The use of the word "story" here in no way implies that people are living in a fantasy world, or that the stories people construct are whimsical. Rather it implies that we construct stories to make sense of our experiences and that the meanings these stories hold can point the way to how we can go on in our lives. I therefore began to conceive of the different psychological theories of death and bereavement that I was using at that time as one set of narratives, and I became interested in exploring alternative death stories to help me evolve new ways of talking to families about death and about mourning. I also began to invite people attending my courses on death and dying to share their own personal and professional ideas about death. In Chapter Two I review a selection of the theses about death and dying that my colleague, Sue Krasner, and I generated with course participants.

Having elaborated my own repertoire of ideas about death and dying beyond those incorporated within the developmental psychology theory of a mature concept of death, I went on to place developmental and psychological theories about death and mourning alongside other conceptualizations of death—for example, cultural, religious, or philosophical. Rather than elevating one set of theses to truth status, therefore, I approached them all as neither right nor wrong ways to believe about death, but as different ways of perceiving.

Everyone has to anticipate the possible future death of parents, friends, and parts of themselves. Having to explain death to children challenges the adult to have to bring into the open ideas and beliefs that she or he may never have had to articulate before. In Chapter Four I explain how I work with families to explore their own beliefs about death and mourning. Following on from the idea that we live our lives according to the stories we tell ourselves, I reflect on how people approach a therapist for help with creating new or alternative stories when the story that they are living by no longer fits with their circumstances, thus leaving them feeling unhappy or disconnected. I present case examples of the clients who came to see me because the stories that they were living and telling about death and mourning were incompatible. Here I explore with clients and professionals their past and current stories about death and mourning, considering not so much "what to say" or "how to say it" but rather "what are the range of possible views" and "what are the implications of particular choices". Moving away from the idea that there is a hierarchy of theories, with some (usually professional) more worthy than others of respect, attention, and "truth" status, I now approach all theories as potential "knowledges" (White & Epston, 1990) that take their place among other "knowledges"—cultural, religious, communal, or personal. Instead of identifying any particular theory, narrative, or discourse as the best way to work or think, therefore, I invite others to evaluate the different theses with me according to their personal and professional contexts. Thus in Chapter Four I use the ideas about death, mourning, and bereavement from Chapters Two and Three as more or less useful in creating with the child and family preferred stories about death and dying that fit more comfortably with their contexts. In this way I see myself and clients as "knowledge-makers" (Epston & White, 1990), who construct our knowledges in relationship with each other, including our families, communities, cultures, religions, professions, and training.

In Chapter Four I also outline the principles guiding my work with children, families, staff, and colleagues as presented in this book. These are informed by the systemic approach (Boscolo, Cecchin, Hoffman, & Penn, 1987) and involve creating a non-evaluative atmosphere; generating and elaborating a repertoire of stories about death and mourning; addressing the fit of different stories between people and with contexts, such as place, time, culture, religion; co-constructing preferred stories with significant people involved; reflecting on the effects and meanings of new stories for individuals and relationships; and translating the stories into action. In Chapter Five I use these principles to co-evolve actions, involving rituals and ceremonies, with bereaved people that make sense of their losses and are coherent with their significant relationships and stories.

In the fifth chapter, I also challenge the view that memories are fixed and stable, and I explore the perspective that they are context-dependent, malleable, and subject to alteration. Hence I introduce an approach to coordinating memories with clients and staff groups that involves re-membering the past into the present to enable people to create a context from which they can go on. Transcripts of my work with families and staff show how this process of "co-memorating" creates an opportunity for the bereaved to revisit old selves and evolve new selves through sharing and creating stories that incorporate the deceased.

Chapter Six reviews the theses and practices presented in this book in the context of training and supervision. Readers are invited to participate in the training exercises outlined with a view to elaborating their stories and conversations about death and dying, valuing their abilities, and extending their practices for working with the dying, the bereaved, and their significant networks. The chapter also addresses the risks and benefits of knowing and uncertainty for people working and training with death and bereavement.

Throughout this book, I take the view that people's beliefs provide useful resources for guiding death talk and mourning practices. In the sixth chapter, therefore, I describe an approach that enables participants in training, supervision, or consultation to become observers to their own beliefs so that they can go on to use them as a resource in conversations with children and families.

I met with the clients in this book in different contexts—at the bedside, on hospital wards, in outpatient hospital clinics or local child and family consultation centres, and on the telephone. In some circumstances I was able to videotape or audiotape sessions, with the consent of all those directly involved. Most frequently I was required to work on my own, but where possible I invited colleagues or trainees to assist me as team members and note-takers during the session, either sitting in the room or behind a one-way mirror. Sometimes I recorded dialogue from memory immediately after the session and at times would ask clients during the session if I might write down a particular phrase, expression, word, or idea.

Case vignettes and transcripts of sessions with clients are presented throughout. In order to ensure that these people cannot be recognized by others, I have changed their names and other potentially identifying characteristics. In some situations I have merged families or combined the experiences or reports of different people to construct one composite case. This approach is intended to protect confidentiality further. For the reader who wants to follow a composite case through the book, Appendix C contains the "names" and the corresponding chapters and pages in the text, together with a brief summary of the child and of the family circumstances.

For the sake of clarity, I have lightly edited the dialogue presented here. I have also in the process removed some of my own ramblings, mutterings, false starts, and hesitations, and so my communications might come across as far more fluent, articulate, and well-thought-out than occurred in the actual situations.

The reader will notice that I have inserted a hyphen between the prefix and the root of some words in the text—for example, "re-member". I have used this technique to invite the reader to take a second look at the word, to see or hear it differently, so that this different perspective and emphasis might create an opportunity for new meanings to emerge. For example, I separate "inter-action" to connote both communication and *action between* people in relationship; "in-forming" to create a sense of both making known to and *bringing into being of* individuals; "(ac)knowledge" to highlight knowledge; "co-memorate" to imply creating memories *with*; and "re-member" to emphasize reconnection with people and to distinguish different ways of using memory from "re-call" and "re-collect". The words "privilege" and "foreground" are used as verbs connoting *make the highest context, highlight,* or *emphasize,* and I use "knowledges" in the plural to reflect the multiplicity of potential theses, narratives, and discourses that we construct to inform our thinking and action.

My approach

It is not my intention to present here a picture of how things are, or a recipe for how they should be done. I have tried instead to put forward a range of theories and stories about death, loss, and bereavement as an invitation to thought and conversation about their connection with practice and action.

My approach is informed by communication theories, social constructionism, and the approaches of systemic family therapy. In particular I draw from the works of the social anthropologist and philosopher Gregory Bateson (1972, 1979), the communication theorists Paul Watzlawick, Janet Beavin, and Don Jackson (1967) and Vernon Cronen and Barnett Pearce (Cronen & Pearce, 1985; Pearce, 1994), and the systemic therapists Gianfranco Cecchin (1987; Cecchin, Lane, & Ray, 1992, 1994), Luigi Boscolo (Boscolo et al., 1987), Tom Andersen (1995), and Michael White (1989). I apologize in advance should my use or applications of their work or the attributions of any of my ideas to their original thinking or practice seem inappropriate or incongruous. However, I also anticipate that those authors will recognize that this book is written within the spirit of postmodern thinking, which acknowledges that our interpretations are influenced by the contexts from which and into which we act, thereby generating the potential for a multiplicity of perspectives.

Throughout this book, I take the position that there is no one correct way to think about death, dying, or mourning, and hence I treat all ideas as hypotheses that are neither right nor wrong but more, or less, useful. In this respect I am influenced by the systemic approach as described by Boscolo et al. (1987). Taking a "not-knowing" position (Anderson & Goolishian, 1992) in relation to clients' beliefs and actions is intended to enable the systemic interviewer to *adopt a non-evaluative stance* and hence remain curious (Cecchin, 1987) about, and connected with, the clients' meanings and stories. Rather than giving advice or interpretations informed by their own preferred hypotheses or theories, systemic interviewers intend to ask questions that closely follow the clients' feedback, in an attempt to explore the clients' preferred theses and explanations, and thereby *generate multiple views.*

The use of relationship questions, rather than statements or suggestions, is central to the systemic method (Tomm, 1988). I therefore ask questions about *relationships* between people and between versions of one's self. I also ask questions about the *differences* between people's views and between contexts. News of difference is intended to introduce new information (Bateson, 1979) to the interviewee and thereby create opportunities for new meanings to emerge and for possibilities of change. The choice of language and the juxtaposition of certain questions also introduce new information into our conversations and enable clients and me to make new connections. It is intended that clients become observers to their own thinking, actions, and contexts in the process of considering their answers to systemic questions. My questions, which address the *effect* or consequences of beliefs on actions or relationships, or of relationships on actions or beliefs, invited the people in this book to look at themselves and their situations from different perspectives.

In the course of the book I take different personal positions in relationship to the material. Therefore at times I speak with my voices of family and culture in relation to my own loss or grief. At other times I narrate with my professional voices, in roles as helper, trainer, supervisor, or consultant. There are times when the voices merge or diversify to encompass or become co-learner or co-traveller. I therefore move between references to "clients", "carers", "professionals", "people", "patients", "colleagues", "participants" in an attempt to reflect the relationship that has emerged in the course of a particular episode of communication.

You, the reader, may choose to take different positions during your reading of this book. For example, you may elect to read from the perspective of a bereaved person, or of a carer of someone who is bereaved or dying; you may also choose to read from the position of a person offering consultation or receiving supervision. This book is therefore intended for people who work with the dying or bereaved, as well as for those whose interest lies in exploring their own understanding about death and bereavement or extending the range of conversations that they might have about dying and mourning. Thus the approaches described can be used by parents with children, helpers with families, consultants with staff, and professionals in training, supervision, or consultation.

DEATH TALK

CHAPTER ONE

To talk or not to talk

Why talk?

Books on death and dying commonly emphasize the necessity for families of the dying to talk about the impending
death with each other. Advice is given to families and professionals to talk openly with the dying rather than indulge in a
"mutual pretence" that he or she is not going to die. It is commonly
suggested that this "mutual pretence" is associated with a poor
dying outcome—for example, a painful or unhappy death for the
dying person, in some cases involving a physical or emotional
struggle. People who are able to talk openly and freely about their
death are deemed more likely to have a "peaceful" death. Links are
also made between the bereaved person's failure to talk about
the death, his or her "denial" of the loss, and a poor prognosis for
resolution of the grieving process. Experts in the field argue that a
satisfactory resolution of bereavement involves "working through"
the loss, which requires talking about it in order to "make the loss
real", "saying goodbye" to the deceased, "letting go", and thereby
being able to "move on" (Worden, 1991).

Established wisdom has it that death talk is a taboo in "our culture", that although we may once have had the ability to talk about death, as a consequence of industrialization and socialization we have lost the capacity to do so, so that "Westerners", at least, are not very good at it. Overtly or covertly the message is that there is a right way and a wrong way to talk about and respond to death and dying.

Hence we receive a set of contradictory messages from professionals that we must talk about death or dying since this is essential for a good death and bereavement and yet that we are no good at death talk, that we don't know how to do it. When confronted with the loss of a significant person, then, not only are we required to manage and make sense of those natural, biological responses to the loss, such as shock, numbness, fatigue, confusion, a pining sort of restlessness with an urge to search for the deceased (Parkes, 1972), we also find ourselves faced with the impossibility of responding to this contradictory set of messages, or double bind—"you must talk but you can't".

Understandable responses to this no-win situation include freezing, avoiding the subject altogether, feeling useless, or giving up. Sometimes we describe these responses as feeling "depressed" or "deskilled".

Recently I was teaching a group of nurses on "Care of the Dying Child and Family". This came towards the end of their rather gruelling course on terminal illness, in which, they told me, they had had "death thrown at us from every angle". An insightful and sensitive participant asked me, "Do you have to be able to talk about death to work with the dying and bereaved?" To this question, I superficially answered "Yes", and then noted a heavy atmosphere come over the room, with a great deal of sighing. Considering my own insensitivity at that moment, I wondered if this was yet another example of having death thrown at them, or had I placed them in a double bind by saying "you must talk" when previous trainers had left them with the message "you can't talk". I tried to redress the balance by clarifying that "Most of us are raised to embrace life and so we become skilled at 'life talk'. Death talk is perhaps a different sort of conversation we acquire through practice. And doing more of it makes us feel more confident with it." I was interested to see the change in atmosphere in the room, and what followed was enthusiastic and creative discussion about the possible ways in which opportunities might be made available to practise conversations about death, like "learning a new language", "death talk evening classes", "talk-ins on death", and "death education in schools".

Well-meaning professionals or concerned family members who are committed to helping their family or patients live well, die well, and grieve well tend to deal with the "must talk, can't talk" dilemma by withdrawing from the situation altogether and passing it on to a specialist. There is a widespread view that death talk is the domain of the experts, requiring training and professional experience, and that those who have not experienced the loss of a loved one are particularly unqualified to partake in this sort of conversation.

Shortly before I wrote this chapter, Emmah Gumede died. She was a woman in her 70s who was responsible for my child care in Africa from the time of my birth until I left home at the age of 17. I heard of her death when I was six thousand miles away from where she lived and died. Disconnected from her world, her people, and her continent, I desperately felt the need for contact with those who knew her. I made a long-distance call to a close childhood friend who had shared with me the warmth, generosity, humour, and being of Emmah. I had hoped to talk and talk and talk about her, those parts of her we knew together, our memories of her. I received a sympathetic response from someone who was somewhat numbed, perhaps by the sudden shock of the news. In my grief I spoke of my loss of direction, an absence of any purpose to my life then, a confusion as to who I was. My friend, perhaps confused by her own grief, or constrained by the context of a long-distance call or frightened by my distress, suggested that I seek therapy.

For a friend or family member, a solution to the "talk but you can't" predicament might include the view that "death talk is a job for the professionals". For the professionals, however, an alternative solution is required. Saying "I don't know what to say" or "I don't know how to say it" or "I find this too upsetting" "or "I don't want to talk to this person" is not a good-enough reason for referral to a specialist. Specialists by definition deal with special cases, with problems. If "not talking" is seen as a problem—for example, as a symptom called "denial" or as a precursor to "pathological be-reavement" and a poor resolution of the grieving process which if not treated would inevitably lead to mental illness—this "problem" could provide the justification for a professional to refer on to a specialist.

> Mr and Mrs D lost their long-awaited first test-tube baby when he was 24 days old. The paediatrician referred the couple to me because Mrs D was "crying every day for a month". I began my preparations for their first session with two assumptions: that this couple had a problem related to their bereavement and that talk-ing about the loss would ameliorate their problem. Consequently, when I met with Mr and Mrs D, I asked them about their loss. They answered my questions willingly and honestly. However the ses-sion felt more like a stilted question–answer exchange, resembling a traditional medical diagnostic interview, than a therapeutic en-counter. When I eventually asked Mr and Mrs D what they thought of their referral to a psychologist, Mrs D said that she had felt nervous before coming and that she was not sure what they were supposed to say here. Mr D asked if other people in their situation reacted in a similar way.
>
> *Glenda:* What do you think about the ways you are responding at the moment?
>
> *Mr D:* I am all right really—well I don't show it so much—I also have work to distract me.
>
> *Glenda:* And Mrs D?
>
> *Mrs D:* I can't stop crying.
>
> *Glenda:* What effect is that having on you?
>
> *Mrs D:* Sometimes it's a relief, sometimes nothing.
>
> *Glenda:* Are either of you concerned about Mrs D crying or Mr D not showing so much at the moment?
>
> *(Mr and Mrs D both shake their heads.)*

Glenda: Is anyone else concerned?

Mrs D: I think Dr K is, because she told me to see you.

Glenda: Concerned about what?

Mrs D: That I am abnormal or something . . . (*grimaces*)

Glenda: Is anyone else concerned—like your family?

Mr D: Both our parents are elderly. This would have been their first grandson. We can't upset them at their age—my mother is not a well woman, and Peg's mum has the strain of her father's condition.

When I first meet with clients I usually begin by clarifying whose idea it was for them to come to see me and who, if anyone, is defining the situation as a "problem" (Palazzoli, Boscolo, Cecchin, & Prata, 1980). With this couple, however, I had immediately launched into the "problem" as defined by the paediatrician, Dr K, without clarifying whether this was at all a concern for either Mr or Mrs D. If I had continued with this approach there is a good chance that between Dr K and myself—and with the couple's compliant view that "professionals know best"—we could have "created" a "problem needing therapy" (Anderson, Goolishian, & Winderman, 1987). People often come for help not because they cannot manage their grief, but because those around them cannot cope or because they are concerned about the effects that they are having on other people. When asked, Mr and Mrs D were able to tell me that their grieving was not a problem for them at that time. They also explained how they could not talk with their family because they felt that they should protect them.

Meanings and messages of death talk

People have a wide variety of different beliefs about death talk. When I began telling people about the subject of this book I was met with a range of responses, from "that's a conversation killer" to disclosures of personal losses and congratulations that I was open to talking and writing about the subject. A commonly held belief is that to talk about death depresses people or spoils the social atmosphere. Many clients have told me that they have purposefully lied about losing a child for fear of causing or being a social embarrassment. The corollary of this "death talk is morbid" belief is that one who listens to death talk is obliged, as a sign of respect, to respond with sadness or silence.

> *Ms H:* I was at a coffee morning with a whole lot of women I had never met before. They were all talking about the strain of having two children. This woman Amanda turned to me and said, don't have a second child, it's a different number. I smiled sweetly. How could I say I have two children but one of them is dead?
>
> *Glenda:* What would happen if you said that?
>
> *Ms H:* I'd ruin the atmosphere—and no one would say anything, be interested.
>
> *Glenda:* What effect did it have on you not saying so?
>
> *Ms H:* I hated myself and them—it's like I said that Georgie never existed and they didn't want to know.
>
> *Glenda:* So you feel you can't get it right—if you talk about Georgie you'll kill the atmosphere; if you don't you kill him off as if he never existed?
>
> (*Ms H, crying, nods.*)
>
> *Glenda:* Do you think people would be interested in hearing about the life of Georgie?
>
> *Ms H:* Huh?
>
> *Glenda:* I mean, here you talk a lot about Georgie as he lived— not just as he died—like the games he played with those marbles and . . .
>
> *Ms H:* (*laughs*) . . . I don't know. They may think death cancels out the good things . . .

An individual can simultaneously hold many beliefs about talking about death. Ms H shows how she entertains a range of beliefs, many of which are contradictory. She believes that not to talk about her son is to deny his existence, as though he never mattered; to talk about him, however, might upset people or "cancel out the good things". It is not uncommon for one person to hold a number of contradictory beliefs, as Ms H does, with the effect that they find themselves torn between responding to these differing views.

We draw our beliefs from the many different situations or contexts in which we operate—for example, our relationships, our past experiences, our families, our own culture, the dominant culture in which we live, our religion, our education, our professions, the law (Pearce, 1994). We carry around with us different messages about talking. Ms H, for example, at one level wants to talk about her dead son when she considers herself in relationship with Georgie; then, not to talk would be to behave as if he does not matter and she would see herself as an uncaring mother. But at a different level, when she thinks of herself as a member of the coffee morning, she does not want to talk; to talk would then be to depress people or be morbid and anti-social. She also refrains from talking when she has the belief that talking about the death cancels out the good things, perhaps even the good things about Georgie. That belief or message may come from another context, such as her culture, which may hold views like "death is a private matter" or the very "words of death have power over life". I have seen people respond to such commonly held beliefs by silently mouthing words or miming actions associated with death or terminal illness rather than voicing them.

Ms H's situation illustrates how one person can hold a number of contradictory views about death talk. The T family below show how, in a similar way, members of a family can hold a range of different or contradictory beliefs.

Mrs T was referred to me with her 9-year-old twin boys, Daniel and Benjamin. The boys' father had died five months previously. Mrs T complained that Daniel was talking incessantly about his father's death; he was also waking at night and could be heard chattering at length to his father, insisting that his father was talking to him. Benjamin, on the other hand had not mentioned his father at all since the boys were told three days after the funeral of his sudden and unexpected death. The boys were away at boarding school at the time, and Mrs T had not wanted to upset them. Distraught herself, she thought they were better off at school not knowing, until she felt in a fit state to tell them. Both boys were furious that they had not been told immediately. Mrs T was still unsure how to talk to her sons about their father's death and came for help with that question. She was attending spiritualist meetings but was unsure whether she "believed"; her family did not approve of this, and she did not want the boys to attend.

It may be that Daniel and Benjamin's responses to their father's death reflect the range of beliefs about death talk in the T family. Daniel's behaviour may reflect their mother's curiosity about communicating with or staying connected to their dead father or her view that the time is right to talk. Benjamin's silence may reflect the mother's view that talking about the death can upset people or that it is best to say nothing until the time is right. His lack of interest in Daniel's conversations with their father might reflect the extended family's disapproval of his mother's interests in spiritualism.

People's failure to converse comfortably with each other about death does not always reflect their lack of ability to do so. In fact, in my experience this is rarely the case. More often, not talking reflects a strong and dominant belief that it is not good, right, or appropriate to talk at that time.

> Mr L was referred to me by the haematologist because he was "refusing to acknowledge" that his 9-year-old daughter was dying of leukaemia. The doctor had tried, on several occasions, to talk to Mr L about the prognosis and complained that he either stared blankly or smiled as if not listening. When I met with Mr L, I did not insist that we talk of his daughter's impending death; instead I asked about his beliefs about death talk.

> *Mr L:* Don't get me wrong. He is a very good doctor. He is treating my girl well. But he thinks I don't know my daughter has leukaemia. He thinks I don't know what can happen. Why is he so worried I should say she will die? What is it for him? For us, we say where there is life there is hope. Monica is still alive—I am not going to kill hope.

Monica's father was responding to a clear and dominant belief that death talk kills hope. It is not unusual for people to believe that death talk is a dangerous thing, that it might welcome or invite death or hasten one's own or someone else's death. A corollary to this belief is that if we don't talk about the death it will go away.

Dina's parents, below, express versions of this belief. Again, their failure to talk about Dina's death with her and with each other does not reflect an inability to do so but, this time, a conflict of beliefs within the family about the meaning of talking about her death and hence what to say.

I was asked by nurses on the paediatric ward to have a word with Dina's mother, Mrs B. Four-year-old Dina had recently been sent home for terminal care. Mrs B was described as "tearful and depressed". She had told the nurses that she could not talk to Dina about dying; the nurses felt Dina was very frightened and that the mother needed help.

Mrs B: Dina asked me, why does life have to end?

Glenda: What did you say?

Mrs B: I just said I don't know, why do you ask? She shrugged and threw a shoe at me. (*Weeping*) Don [her husband] just won't admit Dina is dying. He won't talk about it to me. He keeps going on about Dina's going back to school—it's obscene.

Glenda: What does he feel will happen if he speaks about Dina's dying?

Mrs B: I don't know—it's ridiculous.

Glenda: Do you think his worries about talking to you about it could be similar to your worries about talking with Dina?

Mrs B: How do you mean?—I just can't talk to her about dying.

Glenda: What effect do you think it would have on Dina if you answer her questions?

Mrs B: I can't . . . (*starts blaming her husband again for not admitting Dina is dying and not allowing her to increase Dina's daily dose of morphine*)

Glenda: Would it feel as if you are bringing the end closer if you talked about dying with Dina?

Mrs B: (*crying*) I suppose so.

Glenda: So it may feel as if you would have to start saying good-bye?

Mrs B: (*weeping*) I can't do that, I'm not ready.

Glenda: Do you think your husband is ready yet?

Mrs B: Oh God no—he won't even allow me to increase the damn morphine.

Glenda: What effect does he think increasing the morphine would have on Dina?

Mrs B: Oh that she'll become a druggy . . . she'll be so out of it that she won't be here with us any more.

Glenda: Could his not wanting to increase Dina's morphine be his way of putting off saying goodbye?

Mrs B: He told me he isn't ready yet . . . to talk about it . . . mmm.

Professional with personal beliefs

Thus far we have considered how having different beliefs about death talk might affect the ability and comfort of individuals to enter into conversations about death and dying. The examples I have used emphasize the beliefs of clients and family members. Helping professionals, of course, also hold their own beliefs about death talk, and these influence the ways in which they respond to clients and patients. Each professional will bring to his or her relationship with the client a repertoire of beliefs about death talk drawn from his or her family, culture, religion, professional training. Putting patients, their families, and concerned professionals into the equation, we have on the one hand the potential for a rich resource of ideas about death, and on the other hand the ingredients for conflict between and within individuals.

Most professionals who have attended the bereavement training workshops I have run describe a range of personal beliefs about death and about talking about death. They also describe professional beliefs, reinforced by their training, like those described at the beginning of this chapter, including "it is essential to talk about the death"; "families should talk with the dying member"; the bereaved need to "work through the loss", "make the loss real", "say goodbye to the deceased", "let go", "move on". Often they report that their personal beliefs contradict their professional views. When asked how they resolve the conflicts or contradictions between their personal and professional beliefs when working with patients or clients, helping professionals commonly explain that they prioritize their professional beliefs.

> Nursing Sister Lin on the oncology ward asked me to encourage Mrs W to tell her two children, aged 7 and 11, that she was going to die. She emphasized the importance for this mother and her family that they do this promptly, explaining to me that "Mrs W is more likely to have a comfortable death if she feels she has not left any unfinished business. Also the children need to be prepared or they will be most vulnerable to a pathological bereavement. The family must have a chance to say goodbye so that when the time comes they can work through their loss." I was impressed with Sister Lin's knowledge and experience of work with the terminally ill and the bereaved. Also she clearly had a very close, supportive, and respectful relationship with her patient. I therefore asked her why she did not discuss these issues with Mrs W herself, since her patient appeared to value, trust, and respect her and had confided in her. She explained: "I have two children the same age. In her situation I couldn't possibly tell them. I know exactly how she feels."

It seems that professionals have been encouraged to suspend, in favour of their professional beliefs, the rich variety of ideas that they might bring to their relationships with clients. Sister Lin was not unable to talk with Mrs W. She had the knowledge, she had the skills, she had the relationship with her patient; she also had access to a rich pool of ideas about death talk from which she could draw—her family messages, her cultural stories, her experience as a mother of two children, and her professional training and work with terminally ill patients. However, she experienced these different ideas as in conflict with each other, as if they could not sit comfortably together, but one set had to dominate the other or cancel the other out. Having been trained that good practice requires giving precedence to professional views, Sister Lin recognized her reluctance to act on her professional beliefs with this patient and called me in to talk with Mrs W. Like Georgie's mother, Sister Lin felt caught between opposing messages about how to respond.

After several encounters with talented helpers like Sister Lin, I began to wonder why professionals always elevated the traditional teachings about death talk to the status of "the truth" or "correct way" and why they chose to subordinate the diversity of views and approaches that they had personally lived and experienced, even when the traditional teachings did not fit at all well with their clients' situations. When confronted with this point, a number of helpers argued that it is unethical to "impose your own views" on patients or clients. Raising professional theory and practices over personal approaches therefore might be seen as a protection for patients and clients. Theories about death talk come to function as policy, procedures, and guidelines for good practice, a code of ethics to protect patients from professionals' attempts to dominate them with their own personal, religious, or cultural beliefs. Although possibly not intended, the message seems to have come across that it is legitimate to impose ideas on clients if they come from one's professional training but that it is unethical to impose ideas that derive from one's culture, religion, family, or personal experience.

Talking about death and dying is undoubtedly a very unsettling and emotionally demanding task for most people, professional and public alike, and one develops a number of ways to protect oneself from the pain of entering into the suffering of others.

When I first started working on a paediatric ward that specialized in the treatment of children with life-threatening illnesses, I found myself, one day, walking around the ward at great speed, as if on an important reconnaissance mission. After I had circled the eight-roomed ward three times without stopping, I began to realize that my intention for doing so was not at all clear to me. On reflection, this apparently purposeless behaviour of mine could be understood as my attempt to protect myself from the pain and suffering on the ward; a small child had died on the ward that morning, and patients and staff had recently been informed.

This sort of distraction activity is commonly referred to as a "defence against anxiety" (Menzies, 1959), and in my case I was perhaps "defending" against the anxiety of talking about the death that morning. Theory tells us that we have available to us a number of different defences against anxiety (Freud, 1916–17), and I return to a broader discussion of defences in Chapter Three. Here I am suggesting that elevating professional theories about death over personal theories might be another sort of "defence", a means for professionals of protecting themselves from the pain associated with talking about death. By adopting a professional theory about death talk and turning it into guidelines for good practice, a modus operandi, helpers are protected from having to consider what they themselves believe about death and from having to evaluate their own position against that of their clients. If Sister Lin had used her personal beliefs about death talk with Mrs W, she might have considered her personal experience as a mother of two children and her family or cultural beliefs about talking with children about dying; she probably would have experienced the pain of Mrs W's predicament. By emphasizing her professional beliefs that Mrs W "must talk", she was more likely able to avoid that pain, "know" what to do, and tell herself that she was following good practice.

Death disempowers helping professionals, particularly those of us whose training has led us to believe that we can overcome death by good medical practice or that we can overcome the pain and awfulness of death by good pre-death counselling. Helpers faced with the sense of failure and lack of power commonly described when confronting the death of a patient are perhaps most vulnerable to being seduced by the empowerment of specialist death knowledges—those professional theories and approaches that tell us what should happen and what is the correct way to respond. Elevating his or her professional beliefs, and thereby using specialist knowledges and associated esoteric languages about death and mourning, empowers the helper providing status as expert and consequently disempowers the client.

Talk about talking

Instead of perceiving personal beliefs as obstacles to be subdued or eradicated when working with clients, I am suggesting that helpers might use their own beliefs about death and dying derived from their families, their experience, their relationships, their religion, and their culture as a resource to facilitate their conversations with the dying and bereaved.

During my meeting with Dina B's mother, I reflected on my own beliefs and experiences of talking about death drawn from different contexts including my family, my culture, and the teachings of my professional training. I identified a number of apparently contradictory ideas of mine including, "talking about death helps the dying feel less isolated"; "everyone must mourn" ; "talking is painful"; "it is better to mourn with other people"; "mourning rituals are helpful"; "talking is pointless since it cannot bring the deceased back". I anticipated that one of my dominant professional beliefs—"Adults should respond directly and honestly to the terminally ill child's questions about death and dying"—might predominate during the conversation. I considered what effect it could have on Mrs B if I expressed this belief directly with a comment like "You should try and answer her questions, it is better for her, she is asking you to". I hypothesized that I might undermine Mrs B, increase her guilt, and deskill a mother so committed to the best interests of her child. Instead of discarding this "must talk" belief, however, I decided to add it to my pool of beliefs about death talk and use it as a resource (Cecchin, 1987). I was not going to treat it as a "truth" or the "correct way", but neither was I going to reject it. By taking this "must talk" belief as a starting point and then addressing it from different perspectives, I could contemplate the advantages and disadvantages of talking about Dina's death for each member of the family. Instead of imposing my own professional belief on Mrs B, then, I was able to use the "must talk" belief to guide my conversation with her about death talk with Dina and enable her to think more broadly about her situation so that she might come to an understanding and decision about death talk which better fitted her, Don, and Dina.

In Chapter Six, I describe in more detail how helpers might become observers to their own beliefs about death and mourning and use them as a resource for conversations with others about death and dying. Below I use one of my own beliefs about death talk to inform my conversation with Ms J about talking of the death of her baby, Tyrone.

Ms J had lost her twin baby, Tyrone (3 months), a cot death. She attended her first appointment with her three remaining children, Tyrone's twin sister Tonisha, Nicole (8 years), and Marisa (2 years).

Glenda: Whose idea was it that you come today?

Mother: Dr S suggested it.

Glenda: Any idea what Dr S hoped you would get out of coming?

Mother: To talk to someone maybe.

Glenda: What did you think you might talk about?

Mother: What happened with Tyrone.

Glenda: What did happen?

Ms J. related the circumstances of the baby's death. I included the children in the conversation and asked about the effects of Tyrone's death on all of them. Ms J seemed disengaged from the conversation, answering the questions mechanically. Nicole was eager to discuss what happened and how Tyrone's death was affecting things for her and her family. Marisa kept bringing me toys and stroking my arm. I began to be aware that I was feeling that I could be of no help to this family, that perhaps this sort of session was premature. I was also aware that I was feeling over-whelmed by Ms J's sadness and distracted by Marisa's constant advances. I identified one of my beliefs that "families should be left to get on with their grieving in the early days following their loss". Instead of responding to this belief as if it were a "truth", however, which might have meant remaining in silence or ending the conversation and closing the session, I decided to use this "no point in talking" belief as a resource to guide my conversation with Ms J.

I decided to **talk about talking about the death** of Tyrone. Hence I invited Ms J to reflect on her **experiences of talking about the death**.

Glenda: Who have you spoken with about Tyrone dying?

Mother: Only my friend, Bernice—no one else is interested really.

Glenda: How has talking with Bernice made things?

Mother: She can understand—she lost her baby two months ago. We were on the Special Care ward together.

Glenda: What has helped her to understand—that she has been through it herself?

Mother: Mmm . . . (*nods*)

I was interested in how Ms J experienced the **effects of talking about the death on herself.**

Glenda: Has talking with Bernice been helpful?

Mother: She listens—no one is really interested. The neighbours avoid me or they ask where the baby is.

Glenda: How has having someone to listen helped?

Mother: I can talk about it instead of it going round in my head—and I don't feel so mad.

I went on to explore how she perceived the **effects of death talk on others and on relationships.**

Glenda: How has talking with Bernice made things between the two of you?

Mother: What d'you mean?

Glenda: For example, has it made you closer to each other, do you spend more time together, or has it sometimes felt a bit tense?

Mother: We are much closer.

Glenda: How has it made things between you and the children?

Mother: It's the same.

Glenda: Do you think talking with me could help if I have not lost a baby?

Mother: I don't know. Talking won't help Tyrone.

Glenda: No . . . and that's the most important wish you have at the moment—to have Tyrone back . . . and I can't help with that.

Mother: Mmm . . . (*stares blankly*)

Glenda: Is there anything else you think talking might be useful for?

Mother: I don't know about the children . . . what to say to them. Nicole keeps asking questions; Marisa doesn't understand: she thinks Tyrone is still in the hospital.

By talking about talking about Tyrone's death, Ms J and I were able to clarify the meaning of talking for her and the situations in which she might want to talk with me. Helping professionals sometimes assume that the bereaved need to or want to talk with them. By **exploring alternative relationships for talking**, however, we were able to clarify that Ms J preferred to talk to her friend Bernice in relation to her own feelings because they had shared a common experience. She thought I could help her think about what to say to her children. I could have gone on to **explore other contexts for talking** with Ms J—for example, what she might feel were good times or places for talking. In retrospect I also wonder whether Ms J was unsure about how helpful I might be, not only because I had not shared her experience of losing a child, but perhaps also because I did not share her experience of being a black woman in Britain. If I had considered the context of ethnicity at that time, I may have explored with Ms J how she thought our racial and cultural differences might affect my ability to help her and her family following Tyrone's death, what I would need to know or understand in order for talking with me to feel worthwhile, and whether there were areas in which I might be more or less helpful to the family than other people—for example, her friend Bernice.

When is talking not talking and when is not talking talking?

This reminds me of a riddle I used to ask when I was a child: "When is a cup of tea not a cup of tea?" I used to roar with laughter whenever I gave the reply, "When it is a little sweet", having absolutely no idea what the joke was but enjoying the fact that I was sharing a joke with the usually bemused or bored adult. I would sit for ages trying to work out what was so funny about a cup of tea being a lollipop—and, anyway, if a cup of tea was a toffee or a lollipop, what did it have to do with being a cup of tea? I had the idea that the connection was sugar, but that was about it. What I was struggling with at the age of 6 (most 6-year-olds today have no problem with this) was the different levels of meaning for "a little sweet"—at the object level it describes a small toffee or a lolly or one of those pink scented round things; at the descriptive level it suggests that the tea has too much sugar in it. And thirty-odd years later I ask the parallel question—when is talking not talking, and when is not talking talking? Again, the solution has something to do with different levels of meaning (Bateson, 1972; Cronen, Johnson, & Lannaman, 1982).

At any time when we are in conversation with another, we are communicating at more than one level. At one level a communication conveys information or content; at another level it conveys a message or meaning (Watzlawick et al., 1967). The message or meaning of a verbal communication can be derived from its context and qualified or elaborated by non-verbal behaviour. When Dina asked her mother "Why does life have to end?", she may have been requesting information about life and death in a general sense. The context that Dina was terminally ill led Mrs B to interpret the meaning of her communication as "Why does my life have to end". By answering, "I don't know, why do you ask?", Mrs B could have been responding at two different levels. At one level she could have been conveying the information that she had no general knowledge about the purpose of death. At another, given her relationship with Dina, her reply may have meant that she had "heard" the message level of Dina's communication and at that moment could not bear to address why Dina's life had to end or that she could not think of one good reason why a child should die.

Talk, then, can be direct at the information level or indirect at the message level. When the nursing staff told Mrs B she should talk to Dina about dying, she said she could not. She, however, told me a story that Dina and her parents used to "play".

They would pretend together that there was a huge hot-air balloon on the lawns of Kew Gardens. Next to it was a beautiful picnic, spread out on a tablecloth. Dina and Mrs B would imagine for hours the different foods placed on the cloth and the games and activities that they would get up to. Frequently her father, Don, would join in the "play", suggesting that Dina could ride her bicycle. Occasionally they would invite Dina's favourite people—

Leonardo Turtle and Kermit Frog. Sometimes they would all go flying in the hot-air balloon. Shortly before Dina died, she insisted on taking the balloon up on her own. Her mother begged to go with her, her father tried to entice her to stay on the ground and ride her bike. Dina was adamant that she was going alone and only she would steer the balloon.

When Mrs B told me this story, I suggested that she and Don had been talking with Dina about her death; that the family had found a means of communication at the message level that they all understood. This may not have been apparent to the nursing staff, who perhaps were unaware of the special picnic "play" or did not share the relationship that the B family had with each other and therefore did not understand the message of their communications.

A few months before Monica died, her father told me that she had begun to talk of their family in Africa. She said she wanted to go to her grandmother, who had died three years previously. In response to this communication Mr L had brought in a family photograph album and he and Monica spent many hours reviewing their family life together.

For Mr L, "where there is life there is hope". Although he was not ready to talk directly about Monica's death, he was not neglecting her need to review her life before she died, make it feel worthwhile, put the pieces into place (Butler, 1968). They were doing this together by going over the photographs.

When two or more people engage in any sort of conversation, they are having to attend to and hold in mind communications at a number of different levels. For example, they are considering the content or information of the communication as well as its meaning or message. They are taking into account both the verbal reports and the non-verbal signals and qualifiers. They are assessing the meanings of the communication in the context of what has just been said, their relationship with each other, and what they know and assume about each other. They are using their own personal beliefs and experiences to interpret what they hear and to guide what they say and the way that they say it. Communication then is a complex process. Add to this the emotive subject content of death, with its associated powerful and profound beliefs, and the complexity of the conversation is further intensified.

In the following chapters, I attempt to identify some of the professional and personal beliefs and theories about death and mourning and explore ways in which one might use them as a resource to facilitate conversations about death. In Chapter Two I address personal and professional theories and beliefs about children and death, and in Chapter Three I look at theories and ideas about the best ways to mourn and die.

CHAPTER TWO

Beyond
a mature concept of death

Thirteen-year-old Margaret told the hospital play specialist that her cousin Virginia had said that she had only three days left to live.

* * *

Four-year-old Dina had two imaginary friends, Skimpy and Squonk, who went with her everywhere. As she helped Squonk into the car one day, Dina informed her mother that Skimpy had died.

These two children were suffering with life-threatening illnesses for which no cure was deemed possible. Their announcements occurred around the time the medical team had decided to stop active treatment and to transfer the child to palliative care. Children often discover their prognosis through their reading of the context and non-verbal communication, which includes the interpretations they make of others' behaviour or of the roles of specific hospital staff and procedures. Margaret probably gleaned a lot of information about her health status from eavesdropping on adult conversations. Dina's awareness of death was probably influenced by the contact that she had with other patients who were dying (Bluebond-Langner, 1978; Kendrick, Culling, Oakhill, & Mott, 1987). Usually the child initiates the conversation about death, perhaps in an attempt to establish who knows what, who is open to talk or tell, and whether it is acceptable to talk about death in this relationship. The child may also be conveying messages like, "I am aware of death, I know I am going to die, can you talk about it, can you manage it?"

Behaviour means and communicates

Children's disclosures, like those above, are often brief and to the point, appearing to come out of nowhere and inappropriate to the ongoing action. When they arise within the context of a recent prognosis of terminal illness, adult carers commonly ask what they should say to the child. In situations like these, the adults usually have a choice of responses, and how they continue is influenced by the meanings they give to the child's communication.

> The play specialist above recognized that her response to Margaret would depend on the meaning she attributed to the child's communication. Weighing up several possible alternatives, she wondered if Margaret wanted her to talk to her cousin, or whether she was asking for information about her own death. She also considered that Margaret was expressing her fears and anxieties about dying and that she was trying to establish who knows what and who is open to talking and telling. Unsure which of the many feasible meanings attributable to Margaret's communication she should act upon, the play specialist felt caught between a choice of several possible responses.

The meanings that we give to a child's communication will depend on the contexts that we use to make sense of the communication. These may include our knowledges or beliefs drawn from our professional contexts about the child's developmental level, concept of death, or prior experience, as well as beliefs from our personal contexts—for example, family, culture, and gender. Therefore the carer who says "I don't know *what* to say" may be meaning "I don't know *which* meaning to choose or which meaning to act upon".

> The play specialist asked Margaret if she would like to make a list of the questions she had in her mind, and together they discussed who might be the best person to answer each question. In this way the play specialist intended to communicate to Margaret that she was willing to hear her concerns and to address them where possible.
>
> Margaret's questions list included: "Will my leg get better? Will I be able to walk again? Will my hair grow again? When can I see my twin brother in Africa? Is Virginia telling the truth? Can I stay in the hospital?"

Together the play specialist and Margaret evolved a context in which the child could feel free to talk about her preoccupations and the play specialist could be comfortable with not knowing all the answers. As well as responding to the information or content of these questions, the play specialist could have gone on to explore the different possible meanings of Margaret's questions by asking, for example:

— Are you wanting to know if your leg will get better? Are you also asking if you will recover from the cancer?

— Are you asking if you can stay in hospital because you want to be here at the moment? Are you also wondering whether you will be well enough to leave the hospital?"

Margaret's response to these sorts of questions could help clarify meanings as well as generate new questions and guide the play specialist towards future actions.

Evolving a context of knowing and telling

Carers and children guide their talk and action according to their beliefs about who knows what and who is open to talking about what. This "context of knowing and telling" evolves in relation to the views that they hold about death, carers' ideas about children and about talking with children about dying, as well as the time, place, and relationships significant to knowing and telling. How carers and children act with each other influences the "context of knowing and telling" and in turn is influenced by that context (see also Figure 1, p. 34, below).

> When Mrs B told me that Dina had announced Skimpy's death, I asked her what she thought Dina was trying to tell her or show her.
>
> *Mrs B:* I think she was trying to test the water again. Do you remember when she threw that shoe at me—when I said I didn't know why a life has to end?
>
> *Glenda:* mmm . . . ?
>
> *Mrs B:* Well, I think she has taken a different angle this time.
>
> *G:* What angle is that?
>
> *Mrs B:* I think she is testing the water again—like you said before, maybe she is trying to find out if I can bear to talk about this with her.
>
> *G:* If you could bear to talk about it, what do you think Dina would be wanting to talk about now?
>
> *Mrs B:* You know, I think she wants to understand what happens when people die—we've avoided the subject up to now.

Here Mrs B sees Dina's communication about Skimpy's death as her attempt to *test the water*, to establish whether her mother is willing to talk to her about dying. This time Mrs B goes on to join Dina in evolving a context of knowing and telling in which Dina is able to ask questions about death and Mrs B communicates her willingness to talk.

> Mrs B asked how Skimpy had died and what had happened to her after she died. Later she went on to ask Dina what it was like for Squonk without Skimpy and what she thought Squonk wanted to know about Skimpy's death; together they discussed what Dina could tell him. Over the weeks, Dina returned with many questions that Squonk had about death, dying, and how to reassure the

people who survived. Finally she told her mother that Skimpy had "come alive again".

When nowadays I am asked to talk with a child about death, I first try to join the child and network of carers in conversations to establish the "context of knowing and telling". I begin with exploring what each significant person "knows" about the child's health status, their recognition of each others' awarenesses, and the beliefs that they all hold about people knowing and telling.

When ward staff asked me to talk with Margaret about her poor prognosis, I set out to explore **who knows what, who wants who to know what, and who believes what about who knows what** by asking her carers:

— What do you know?

— What do you think Margaret knows?

— Where does she get that idea from?

— What have you noticed about her behaviour/relationships recently?

— What does that suggest to you about her understanding?

— What are you doing that is different from how you were before you understood that she is not going to get better?

— What changes might Margaret have noted in her body/how you are/your relationship with her?

— How do you think she might be explaining these changes to herself?

— What experiences has Margaret had of death?

— Who died? What was she told? How did she respond? What sense did she make of it at the time?

— How do you think that has affected her understanding of her own situation?

— What do you think she wants to know?

— What has she said/done that tells you that?

— What do you think (significant others) want her/others to
know?

To establish further a context of knowing and telling with
Margaret, I could have suggested that the play specialist follow
Margaret's earlier questions by asking her :

— How would you answer that question (yourself)?
— Where did you get that idea from?
— Who else do you think has a similar/different view? What do
they think?
— How come you think they see things the same/differently?
— What do you think your aunty knows at the moment? And
your mother?
— What do you think they would like you to know?

Since sharing information with young patients commonly raises
dilemmas for hospital staff (Bluebond-Langner, 1978) and parents
are less likely to acknowledge mutually the approach of death with
their child (Goldman & Christie, 1993), I try to address **when and
whether it would be a good idea to talk** early on in our work
together, with questions like :

— When would be a good time to talk with Margaret about the
future of her (illness/treatment/recovery)?
— How do you know?
— What are the advantages/disadvantages of talking now?
— How would you decide who talks with Margaret (and who
else takes part)?

Even in an open context of knowing and telling, more distancing
and less contact has been noted between the dying child and carers
(Bluebond-Langner, 1978; Rothenberg, 1974), who may avoid the
child's room or make excuses to leave, thereby keeping interaction
with the child brief. I therefore find it useful to raise the issue of

involvement and closeness between carers and children in the early stages of establishing a context of knowing and telling with questions like :

— What effect will talking about this have on you/significant others, and on your relationships (with each other and with the child)?

— Do you think you are likely to spend more or less time with each other?

— Do you think you will be closer or more distant from each other?

— How would *you* prefer it?

— To what extent will you be available to (the family/the child) after (we) have spoken?

The opportunity to refer back to earlier conversations about involvement and closeness has often arisen, especially at times when relationships between the staff, the child, and the family become stressed.

Initially the ward staff insisted that Margaret be told immediately, since they believed that she was already aware she was dying and that she needed to talk. The play specialist believed that telling Margaret about her prognosis would "free her to talk about all the worries on her mind" and enable her to develop a more open and honest relationship with the child. The nursing staff agreed that Margaret would benefit from more open communication, and they were unsure how her knowing might affect their relationships with her. Margaret's foster-mother was reluctant for her to be told since she thought that "the child will go downhill before her mother reaches her". Margaret's family was in Africa. Her mother, who visited three times a year, had left her in London in the care of friends shortly after diagnosis, so that she could receive "the best treatment". Tearfully the foster-mother said she did not know what she could say to her daughter, Virginia, who had become a sister to Margaret and would "never get over this".

Exploring the "context of knowing and telling" revealed Margaret's foster-mother's belief that *not telling equals protection* of Margaret and Virginia from distress, *protection* of the relationship between the cousins, and possibly *protection* of Margaret from deterioration and death. Hence the foster-mother feared that Margaret would give up if she knew how ill she was. Children are often defined as lacking in knowledges, hence requiring both protection and education. Sharing knowledges with children may therefore be seen as enabling their self-protection. However, children are also deemed in need of protection against knowledge. Since the balance between protection and knowledge is particularly pertinent in evolving a context of knowing and telling about death with carers and children, I generally **enquire about protection**. For example :

— What would you want to protect Margaret from?

— What does Margaret need to know so that she can feel protected?

— What would knowing protect Margaret from? How would not knowing protect her?

— What sort of protection could you give to Margaret (and Virginia) if she knew?

— Do you think Margaret is trying to protect anyone?

Children's knowing

When I started working with dying and bereaved children, my approach to a *child's* knowledge and understanding of death was informed by a small literature on children's concept of death, which in turn was informed by theories of developmental psychology (see Appendix A). Implicitly accepting the assumption of a "mature" concept of death as representing the most advanced stage of awareness and understanding, I viewed the younger child's thinking as qualitatively different from that of older children and adults, whom I expected to demonstrate more "adequate" ways of perceiving death. I therefore tailored my talk with children, and the interventions or advice I gave to their carers, to fit with the developmental psychology thesis that young children do not have a mature concept of death. I assumed that adults and adolescents with a mature concept of death would expect "immobility", changed "appearance", and "insensitivity" of the dead person as well as acknowledge that the bodily functions are "dysfunctional", that the "separation" is permanent and "irreversible", and that death is "universal", with a "causality" that may be internal or external (Kane, 1979). In this way, I located the knowledge within the child, thereby focusing on the child as an individual. It was not long before I was so well versed in such developmental stage theories of the concept of death that quite automatically I subjected each child I encountered to my developmental psychology gaze.

When Ms J (Chapter One) said she would like some help with talking to her children, Nicole (8 years) and Marisa (2 years), about the cot death of their baby brother, I was guided by developmental psychology to tell her what her children could know. Drawing her attention to Marisa, who was putting a baby doll under a toy cot, repeating "baby gone, baby gone", I explained that a bereaved child as young as 2 can achieve a basic understanding of death when confronted with a very significant death experience (Furman, 1974). I also explained that Nicole, at her age, was more likely to understand that death is final and may perceive death as an external force, perhaps personified as something like a death person or an angel (Nagy, 1959). I added that children of Nicole's age may not necessarily see death as inevitable and could presume that only the old die (Kane, 1979).

* * *

When Mrs B told me that Dina had informed her that Skimpy had come alive again, her report resonated with my developmental story that the beliefs of children at this age are egocentric and that magical thinking typifies the child (Piaget, 1958). Therefore, supported by my knowledge that most children who are 3 to 5 years old lack an appreciation of death as a universal phenomenon involving a final and complete cessation of bodily functions (Kane, 1979), I explained to Mrs B that at her age Dina was most likely to perceive death like sleep, with the possibility of return to life. In this way she would understand death as merely a temporary and reversible diminution of function. Mrs B gave me time to share my perspective and then went on to tell me that she and her husband were delighted with Dina's report that Skimpy had come alive again since it gave them the opportunity to share with Dina their Buddhist stories about reincarnation.

Mrs B gently challenged my developmental story about children and death and helped me to recognize how I had been seduced by a general psychological model that assumes a standard developmental process and ignores the relevance of culture, religion, race, class, and gender as well as the uniqueness of the dying child's experience. Looking through different eyes at developmental psychology, I began to see it as a normalizing discipline that pathologizes those who fail to meet its models and is unable to make sense of differences except as inferiorities. I reflected on how developmental stage theories had provided me with a lens through which I was observing children, leading me to assumptions of what to expect and, more importantly, what not to expect. Using theories about the intellectual and emotional development of the mythical "normal" child, I was making assumptions about what Dina B could be meaning and what she was incapable of meaning. I failed to consider Dina's experience of the death of a little friend with a similar illness to her own or how her story about Skimpy fitted with the Thai culture and Buddhist religion of her family. Had Mrs B not interrupted my "develological" flow, I might have gone on to construe Mr and Mrs B's cultural and religious beliefs as their defence against looking at the finality of death and hence their avoidance of the actual loss and separation, thereby pathologizing the B family on the basis of their "failure" to reflect the Western, middle-class norms that have structured developmental research.

Beyond a mature concept

When Sue Krasner and I invited professionals to explore their own beliefs about death and dying (see Exercise 1 in Chapter Six), we noted that they shared a wide range of perspectives that did not always conform with a picture of the "mature" concept of death. Drawing from both their personal and their professional contexts, some of their stories about death did embrace the positions identified in the developmental thesis of a mature concept of death, in particular the assertions that death is final, universal, natural, and has a cause. For example, there was general recognition that death is the end of life as we know it, that the body is gone (finality), and that there is always a time to go since death is part of the natural cycle of things (natural and universal). However participants also addressed continuity after death, with stories of after-life, reincarnation, and how the dead live on in the memories of the living, through surviving family members, through genetic transmission, or through peoples' impact on the world. This led to conversations about continuing relationships with the dead, including acknowledging the importance of ancestors, mourning, and rituals. Going beyond the developmental story to explore other stories about death, participants shared thoughts of death as abstract and intangible as well as concrete conceptions of death as "a friend" or "the enemy", and they reflected on death's representation in symbols or artefacts of art or religion. They approached views about the existence of spirit or soul as distinct from body and about heaven and hell, and they exchanged stories about the causes of death, including themes from religion and mythology, medicine and science, as well as nature and fate. Ideas differed about acceptability, and death was seen as a release or welcome relief from pain, as well as hollow and empty, painful and uncomfortable. Death was construed as affecting only those closely related and involved with the deceased as well as a communal affair, so that when someone dies something in everyone dies.

I noted that participants showed more enthusiasm for stories that went beyond the mature concept of death. It was as if, once they had set down the theses (final, natural, universal, inevitable), they could go on to embrace "alter-theses", including continuity and those situations where death was unnatural, specific, and uncommon. Moving beyond the mature concept of death, they could share different stories, both abstract and concrete, about the causality, acceptability, and communality of death.

Participants also reflected that in the context of a *child's* death, their narratives emphasized continuity and privileged the unnatural, uncommon, and specific dimensions as well as non-material explanations of the death. Mr L (Chapter One) reflected this same process after his daughter Monica died, when he told me:

On the day Monica died it was enough to know she died from leukaemia. And when we saw her in the chapel on those days afterwards, I could understand it. But after the burial I wanted more. Saying the leukaemia killed her was not enough. I am still left with the question: why her, why our child, why so young? Then I start to ask, is there a God, what does my life mean now, and why am I still alive?

For Mr L, the "mature" concept made sufficient sense of his daughter's death until her funeral. Once she was buried, however, his questions show how he chooses to go beyond the mature concept to create new meanings.

In the context of a child's death, the thesis identified with a mature concept of death no longer seems to fit. When the death of children is uncommon, people often say that it feels unacceptable to conceive of a child's dying as natural. In this context, then, Mr L and the course participants found themselves going beyond causal explanations with their physical, medical, or natural theses and associated notions of the inevitability, universality, and finality of death, towards philosophical, religious, mythological, or personal stories that address explanations of the motivation or justification of death.

I do not intend to invalidate the developmental psychology thesis here but, rather, acknowledge its place amongst other theories, stories, and ways of making sense of these experiences. Conversations with course participants have helped me to elaborate my own repertoire of stories about death with an extended range of ideas that might be more or less useful in the conversations that I have with children and families. In this way, the developmental stages or levels take their place amongst other conceptualizations about death—for example, cultural, religious, or philosophical— not as *the* right or wrong way to believe about death, but as *ways* of believing. In Chapter Four I show how these different conceptualizations inform the questions that I ask and thereby guide my conversations with families to evolve new stories about death that fit more comfortably with their contexts.

Instead of assuming children's understanding on the basis of the developmental psychology story, I now ask questions about what the children know and what people think they should know. I might offer the developmental story as one thesis and invite families to put forward their own theses, for example:

> There is one theory that tells us that children of Nicole's age do not necessarily see death as inevitable and are most likely to presume that only old people die:
>
> — What do you think of this idea? What would others (family/community) say about this?
> — Do you think it fits for Nicole? What do you think, Nicole?
> — If you were to accept this view, how would you respond to (be with/talk with/understand) Nicole?
> — How would others in your (family/community) view this?

Rather than locating the knowledge in the child, I am interested in how the child's knowledges are being constructed in relationships with their family, culture, community, hospital, and other significant contexts. I have become more curious about the different theses that people hold about children's knowledges and understanding. Thus I would attempt to invite the family and carers to become observers to their own beliefs, feelings, and relationships and to share such observations in our creating a context of knowing and telling.

Identity and relationships

The identities of children and parents are interconnected with the expectation that the child will one day become an adult. For children this involves participation in relationships and institutions that mark them as children and confirm investment in their futures as preparation for maturity. For parents or significant carers this involves taking a key role in nurture, protection, provision for the future, and authority in relation to the child. Dying children, however, will not "become", and in this sense they are seen to have no future. Although they may participate in institutions, like school, which mark them as a child, they cannot be prepared for adulthood. Therefore the child's impending death is a challenge to his or her own sense of self and achievement, as well as that of the carers.

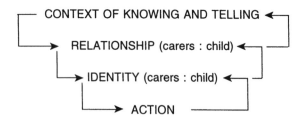

FIGURE 1.   The context of knowing and telling influences identity
and relationships

For the child it can represent failure to become; for parents it may belittle their efforts to protect, nurture, rear, and provide; and for medical staff it can undermine their role in the curing process (Bluebond-Langner, 1978).

Figure 1 illustrates how the relationship between child and carer provides a context for the identity of the child, parents, and hospital staff and how their identities in turn influence their relationships and the way they inter-act. The identity and relationship of child and carers is affected by the "context of knowing and telling", and children and carers inter-act to maintain or change that context.

The play specialist had predicted a more relaxed and honest relationship between herself and Margaret if the child were to know her prognosis; the nursing sister guessed that telling Margaret would make little difference to her relationship with the child. Thus a context of open acknowledgement could confirm the play specialist's identity and reinforce her role to support, entertain, and be available to empathize with the child and enable nursing staff to continue to do what society expects of them by administering medication to ensure that the child is free from pain and discomfort. The foster-mother, on the other hand, was unsure how to go on in her relationship with Margaret should the context change to one of mutual acknowledgement of the child's dying. Unsure of how she could be with a child without a future, she asks what is her role, what is their relationship, what is their future in the face of no future.

Below, I begin to explore with the foster-mother alternative ways of being, other identities for her and the child that do not presuppose Margaret's development towards adulthood, by asking:

— What do you see as your main responsibility/job (as a mother) with your child?
— What effect would her knowing have on this job (your ability to be her mother)?
— If she knew about her dying, how could you/she continue being together?
— How could you still feel you were being a parent/nurture her/ protect her?

> *Glenda:* How do you think telling Margaret that she will not recover from the cancer will make things for the two of you?
>
> *Foster-mother:* . . . and after that, then what are we supposed to do? Do you expect me to carry on like it was all normal again? I can't do that.
>
> *Glenda:* Could you help me understand a bit about what being normal is for you and Margaret . . . and Virginia, too?
>
> *Foster-mother:* You know, we get on with it . . . .
>
> *Glenda:* Could you give me some idea—like what do you all do when you're getting on with it—how does it look?
>
> *Foster-mother:* I get the girls up for school, check they have their packed lunch, get their tea ready, you know. We manage.
>
> *Glenda:* So "normal" is you doing the things the girls need to help them grow up? Like making sure they are fed and educated— you are nurturing them, helping them to grow and develop?
>
> *Foster-mother:* (*nods*)
>
> *Glenda:* And you were telling me earlier on how you have always protected them, made sure they are safe and comfortable and not too upset?
>
> *Foster-mother:* Mmm . . .
>
> *Glenda:* Are you still able to be a mother in this way while Margaret is in hospital . . . . for Margaret I mean?

Foster-mother: Well she can't go to school these days and she picks at her food—but we got some lessons from the teacher, and she still likes my beans (*smiles*).

Glenda: If Margaret knew and understood that treatment cannot help her get better, if she knew that and you knew that, and Virginia knew that—how would you all carry on being together? Would you still bring in her school work and make her beans?

Foster-mother: As I said, she'll give up—like, what's the point.

Glenda: Could you carry on being a mother if she looked like she was giving up?

Foster-mother: How? You tell me . . .

At the moment Margaret and her foster-mother are behaving "as if" she is going to become an adult. Margaret does her school work "as if" she is preparing for a future, and her foster-mother feeds and nurtures her "as if" laying the foundations for her maturity. In the face of a child's death, the child and significant carers often behave "as if" the child will become an adult, so that those involved can continue to fulfil the responsibilities necessary to affirm their identities. Behaving "as if" the child will become offers them a way to do what society expects of them and in this way keeps the parent–child, doctor–child relationship from breaking down.

At times it becomes unworkable to behave "as if" the child will become, especially when the needs of individuals and between individuals come into conflict—for example, when children's need to talk and share their knowledge of their prognosis interferes with their need to have their parents with them, when parents' need to nurture their children competes with their need to protect them from knowledge of the prognosis, and when staff's need to treat children is challenged by their need to see them as able to benefit from treatment. In these sorts of situations, those significantly involved may seek alternative ways of being together.

In Chapter One, Dina B and her parents resolved the conflict between her need to talk and share and their need to protect her from knowledge of her prognosis by communicating obliquely through their shared story about the air balloon. In a similar way, Mr L and Monica reviewed their life together and shared stories about deceased grandparents.

Another solution to this dilemma commonly adopted by medical teams is to allocate one person to talk with the child so that family and carers can continue to relate "as if". I was asked to talk to Margaret about her prognosis, and the play specialist was expected to provide the child with the opportunity to ask questions.

Distancing and silence can also be seen as strategies to maintain relationships and identity without challenging the "as if". For example, parents and carers may avoid the child's room and children may refuse to talk, withdraw, cry, or engage in superficial or inaudible conversation.

Evolving a context of mutual acknowledgement does not automatically ensure open communication, support for the child, or positive outcome for family, child, and staff relationships. In Bluebond-Langner's (1978) study, parents who practised open awareness were as frequently absent from the child, and staff avoided the room as much, as those who practised "mutual pretence". Often staff responded more negatively to these parents, ostracizing them for being bad parents who did not protect their offspring from unhappy news.

> Shortly after Jamie M's parents were told that the leukaemia had returned and that medical treatment could offer no more than palliative care, 10-year-old Jamie stopped speaking of the future plans or goals that had formerly filled him with enthusiasm. He no longer mentioned growing up and showed anger if anyone else did. Unable to act "as if" Jamie was going to become, his parents preferred to acknowledge openly his prognosis with him. When Jamie began to use distancing strategies like silence and withdrawal, his parents sought help as to how they could go on to be with Jamie in the context of shared knowing that he would not become.

Open acknowledgement of the child's dying challenges the identity and relationships of the child and carers, and parents like Mr and Mrs M may ask for help with how to be in the face of their child's death. Psychological theories of development for "normal" children presume a future for the child and presuppose maturity into adulthood. Initially Jamie's parents were at a loss as to how to conceive of their role and relationship with their child who would never reach adulthood. Nursing staff were at a loss as to how to proceed with a child for whom theories of normal development were inappropriate. I therefore invited them to **address how impending death challenged the identities of the child and all those involved** with questions like

— How might we think of Jamie's main job/role in being a child?

— What effect would his knowing have on his view of himself (ability to be a child)?

— How could he still feel he is a child?

— How does Jamie's prognosis challenge our view of ourselves as (doctors/nurses/psychologists)?

This line of enquiry set a context that enabled carers and family to move away from a future framework and provide a present focus for their inter-acting. In Chapter Three we see how parents and carers were able to evolve a way of being with Jamie that involved working together to create a meaningful project in the here and now.

CHAPTER THREE

Getting it right

The perfect death

Mrs H repeatedly referred to her memory of the day that her 6-year-old son Georgie died. She sobbed when she pictured his final breath and what she described as the "fit" that preceded it. Several times she drew for me a powerful image of how "his eyes rolled back in his head, he twitched and shook and went dead and staring, pale and milky . . . his mouth wide open, his eyes glazed". She wept that Georgie had not died peacefully, had not "just floated away . . . why did he have to struggle like that?"

Dying is not always a beautiful affair, and how people die can remain with the memories of the people who live on. The effects of these memories can differ, depending on the theories that the bereaved use to make sense of the episode of death. Beginning with the theory that a good death is a peaceful death, a pain-free death, involving open communication between all family members and honest preparation of the child, Mrs H could only lament the lost opportunity for such a perfect death and criticize herself for not doing the right things to enable it. Feeling a failure that she had not helped her son to have a peaceful and easy death, she experienced his death in terms of a "fit" and a "struggle", which she attributed to her refusal to heed the advice she was given to "let go" and to her difficulty with managing his pain control.

> When I asked Mrs H what she thought Georgie was struggling for, she identified his struggle to stay alive "because he loved his life and he wanted to be with his family". Comforted by this view, Mrs H began to talk of Georgie as the sort of child who did not give up easily, who held on vehemently to what he wanted, "like a dog on a bone", and her memories of his death began to represent, for her, the determination of her son. When she was gently helped to shift her view of Georgie's dying from a "fit" to a "struggle for something" (Watzlawick et al., 1967), his dying took on a different meaning and image for her, so that she began to take the perspective that Georgie had "died in his own way" and "put up the fight" that he, and all her family, were proud of.

Scientific advances in the control of pain have generated many more opportunities for a relatively pain-free death (Goldman, 1994) and for stories about comfortable and peaceful deaths, so that for most people a peaceful death is the perfect death, and a death involving pain and struggle is deemed a failure. I asked a group of nurses and doctors about their roles and responsibilities with dying patients. The doctors unanimously stated that their responsibility was to prevent death and acknowledged overwhelming feelings of failure if patients died. They added that in cases where the death was "inevitable" they were responsible for controlling death: slowing it down and balancing pain control with death control. They were clear that it was possible to get that balance right or horribly wrong, and a number of them were keen to perfect the control. The nurses emphasized comfort of patients and their responsibility to alleviate pain and fear. They, too, recognized their commitment to getting it right.

Many hospitals have set up committees to develop procedures and standards for good practice to guide professionals towards getting the process of patients' dying right. The procedures informing good psychological and emotional practice are commonly drawn from psychological theories of death and bereavement.

The right ways to die and grieve

At times of despair and confusion, a theory that fits—be it religious, cultural, or psychological—can offer guidance, clarity, and the security of a way to proceed. When it does not fit, however, it can leave one at best still in a state of despair or confusion, at worst feeling criticized, mad, bad, or abandoned.

> Sister Lin, whom we met in Chapter One, told me that she had been to a week's course on "Working with Death and Dying", where she had learnt about stage theories of dying and bereavement (Bowlby, 1980, Kubler-Ross, 1970). From this course she had drawn the knowledges to inform her work with Mrs W, who had been dying from cancer. Sister Lin expressed considerable dismay that Mrs W had died while "still in the bargaining stage"; she believed that she had not approached Mrs W in the right way and therefore had "spoilt" her death for her and her children. She felt that she had "failed" her patient by not helping her to work through the stages of denial and isolation, anger, bargaining, and depression, so that she could "reach the acceptance stage, without feeling depressed or angry, and so die peacefully".

From talking with nurses, psychologists, doctors, and social workers, I have learnt that professionals have commonly responded to Kubler-Ross's (1970) stages of dying by expecting and in many cases "helping" dying people and their families to negotiate the stages as she listed them (see Appendix A). On a number of occasions I have been asked to see a client or family to help them "express their anger" or conversely to help a client described as angry to "move on and come to acceptance" of the death.

> Recently I was asked by a colleague in a supervision session to help her assess whether a client had "emotionally processed" the death of her child.
>
> *Glenda:* Have you asked her?

Colleague: Asked her what . . . I mean what could I say?

Glenda: Well, what would you want to know . . . what do you mean by emotionally processed?

Colleague: Has she got over it, is it still interfering with her life.

Glenda: And?

Colleague: . . . has she achieved the tasks of mourning—I don't find the stage and phase theories of mourning very helpful—too passive.

.Whereas Kubler-Ross (1970) describes stages of mourning, both Parkes (1972) and Bowlby (1989) propose that the person must go through series or phases before mourning is finally resolved (see Appendix A). These phases include experiences like numbness, yearning, denial of the permanence of the loss, anger, disorganization, despair, and reorganized behaviour. For Bowlby mourning is finished when the person completes the final restitution phase. My colleague explained that to her, the stage or phase theories imply a passive passage through time, with little opportunity for the dying or bereaved personally to influence the grieving process. She preferred to think of the mourner as having to achieve certain tasks, thereby implying that mourners need to take action and have personal agency in the process of mourning. Together we developed a range of questions that she might ask her client, to address the extent to which she had negotiated four tasks: acceptance of the reality of the loss, working through the pain of the grief, adjusting to the environment in which the deceased is missing, and, finally, moving on with life. My colleague and I met later to review her work with her client.

Colleague: I wanted to know what progress Mrs C was making with working through the pain.

Glenda: How did you explore that?

Colleague: I asked whether she was still feeling that gaping hole in her chest that she described. She said it was still there. I then asked if it was still as large or whether she had managed to reduce its size or intensity. She said, "I don't want to".

Glenda: What effect do you think your questions had on Mrs C?

Colleague: I suppose I went too fast . . . maybe she thought I was trying to take her pain away? I suppose I was, in a way.

Glenda: What ideas do you have about the meaning of Mrs C's gaping hole for her? . . . What effects could its shrinking have on her, her husband, their relationship?

Colleague: I could ask her that—I was probably over-committed to the idea that she had to work through her pain.

Glenda: Did she say her gaping hole was her pain?

Here my colleague and I were helped by Mrs C to question our own beliefs about the process of mourning. My colleague learnt that she was "over-committed" to a task theory of mourning (Freud, 1917; Worden, 1991; see also Appendix A). She realized that she was using the task theory as a normative blueprint of the mourning process against which to evaluate Mrs C's progress. She reflected that she was so "in love" (Boscolo, 1989) with her own bereavement theories that she had not stopped to listen to her client. Letting go of her commitment to these theories, she became increasingly more curious about what the "gaping hole" meant for Mrs C.

Although I never met Mrs C, she has encouraged me to ask clients what *they* consider to be the tasks of mourning, and whether or not they *want* to negotiate such tasks. I now spend more time exploring with them the possible effects of different sorts of mourning on themselves and their relationships including their relationships with family, religion, culture, and versions of themselves and with the deceased. Consequently I have learnt through many conversations with clients about the rich and varied beliefs that people hold about what is the "right" way to mourn and grieve. We explore these in more detail in Chapter Five.

Different sorts of knowing

Professionals have frequently asked me to help their clients to accept death or dying, which involves coming to the belief that reunion is impossible, in this life at least. The opposite of "accepting" is viewed as not believing, through some sort of denial. I have never been asked to help clients or families deny a death, but on several occasions I have been called to overcome "denial". The dominant views that seem to inform most professionals' concerns in this area include that it is necessary to go through pain in order to get the grief work done, and that failing to acknowledge openly a death means that it is outside a person's consciousness. These beliefs are intricately woven with the view that there is a normative blueprint for grieving and that people get stuck in the grieving process if they do not accept the death. Acceptance is therefore viewed as rational, whereas thought of reunion—commonly connoted as denial—is viewed as irrational and a cause or symptom of pathological bereavement, to be dealt with in the interests of clients' future mental health (Black, 1994; Judd, 1989).

> I was asked to help 9-year-old Miriam accept that her 7-year-old sister, Tania, was going to die. Tania had been unconscious for four days, having been recently diagnosed with an inoperable malignant tumour. Miriam had remained by her bedside, talking to Tania, drawing her pictures, and singing her songs. Their mother, a lone parent from Peru, who had only recently come to Britain following the death of the girls' father from cancer, was worried that Miriam was not understanding the situation. She had also been told by her social worker that she should help Miriam to know the truth. When I met Miriam with her mother, she was carrying a drawing for her sister, "Tania on the bed with Angels".
>
> Glenda: Your mother and the nurses are worried that you don't understand that Tania is going to die. What do you think about that?
>
> Miriam: She's sleeping now, she'll be better soon.
>
> Glenda: Are you pretending that Tania will be better?
>
> Miriam: Yes.
>
> Glenda: I see . . . so when will you be able to stop pretending?
>
> Miriam: When all the family come from Peru.
>
> Glenda: So you're pretending for now that Tania will get better? And if all the family comes from Peru then you can stop pretending and then you can think that Tania is going to die?
>
> Miriam: Yes.

The professionals who asked me to help Miriam and her mother were starting from the position that Miriam needed to "know" the "truth". I was asked to ensure her "knowing" in order to ensure her well-being. Miriam was starting from a different position—that there are different sorts of "knowing" and that the sort of knowing she shows or foregrounds is influenced by context. When I first spoke with Miriam, we were in the context of the hospital, her relationships with nursing and play staff, and her mother. She showed me that for her to engage in a different sort of "knowing" about Tania's imminent death she needed the context of extended-family relationships, including aunts, uncles, and cousins from their village in Peru.

A colleague asked me to see a young man who had been diag-nosed HIV positive and had recently been suffering from AIDS-related illnesses. She was concerned how this young man's "denial" might affect his health, and the health of and relationship he had with his partner. I asked her to join me when I met with him and explained to him that my colleague was concerned about his understanding of his illness and had asked me to talk to him about this. I then asked my colleague to clarify her concern. She explained that Colin had told her on several occasions that you cannot die from AIDS. I asked him if he saw it this way. He agreed.

Colin: AIDS can't kill.

Glenda: Have you always had this view?

Colin: No, not always.

Glenda: Was there a time when you thought about AIDS in a different way?

Colin: (*nods*)

Glenda: Do you think you will always have the same view in the future?

Colin: What?

Glenda: Well that you can't die from AIDS—do you think you'll carry on with that view in the future or do you think you may sometimes think about AIDS as you have done before now?

Colin: Probably think different again.

Glenda: Are you choosing to think that you can't die from AIDS for the moment?

Colin: Yes . . . for the moment.

I was asked by nursing staff to help Miriam "know" the "truth" about Tania's death. I was asked by Colin's doctor to ensure he was fully aware of his illness. In both cases, professionals held the view that Miriam and Colin were "in denial" and that the "truth" was outside their conscious awareness. Miriam and Colin, on the other hand, showed me that the contexts of time, place, and relationships influenced the quality and nature of their knowing about death and illness, that different knowledges were more fitting to be "known" in different situations, and that the presence or absence of supporting relationships was an essential ingredient to their (ac)knowledging.

The professionals asking for my help were presenting Miriam and Colin's "denial" as symptoms, inner states, or ways of being. Had I adopted this perspective I may have set out to remove their symptoms, alter their states, or change their ways of being. Instead I began with the perspective that denial was not a part of Miriam and Colin's being nor a state outside their consciousness, but rather a *sort* of "knowing" that they were *showing* in that particular context. Moving away from the view that they were *resisting* the truth of their situations, I saw them as *persisting* for the time being with a particular version of knowing. Seeing Miriam and Colin as embracing several "sorts of knowing", rather than as having no knowledges at all, freed me from pressure to identify the cause of their denial, to remove it, or to fill them with *the* knowledge. Instead I became increasingly curious (Cecchin, 1987) about their different sorts of knowing, which invited a sharing in different kinds of conversation with them.

I asked Miriam and her mother about their family in Peru, the possible differences their presence might make for each of them, their relationship, and their feelings about Tania's dying.

Miriam and her mother spoke about the absence of their large family from their village. They explained the importance of family for the grieving rituals of their culture. This in turn invited stories from Miriam about her father's death, where numerous family members took it in turns to stay around the "dying bed", took part in a wake after the death, and celebrated her father's life with a large family party.

Starting from the perspective that Colin was showing a different sort of "knowing", I became curious about the different sorts of knowing he had access to, to whom he showed which of his knowledges, which situations invited what sorts of knowing, which relationships supported or constrained which (ac)knowledgements, and the possible consequences of the different sorts of knowing.

Colin shared with me and his doctor that a close friend had recently died from AIDS-related illness, and he had not discussed this with his partner who was not HIV positive. This death was preoccupying his mind at the moment. His follow-up hospital appointment had "come at the wrong time", when for him (ac)knowledging his own mortality felt particularly difficult. With Colin and his doctor we were able to explore the possible effects of Colin's choosing not to (ac)knowledge the consequences of his illness at that time. Colin showed how his choosing to not know the probable fatal consequences of his illness inhibited his ability to communicate openly and comfortably with his partner at the moment and thereby interfered with their opportunity to share the grieving for their friend who had just died. His choosing to not know did not interfere with his appropriate use of medication, his care of himself, nor his safe-sex practices. His doctor was able to discuss how his choosing to not know affected her relationship with Colin and that they would need to clarify what sort of knowing he was showing her in the future.

Making emotions

During our bereavement training courses, Sue Krasner and I ask participants to share early memories of grieving and mourning. Many have recalled embarrassment or shame when, as young children, they were not feeling sad or miserable at the death of a relative; or they recounted childhood memories where they had feigned sadness so that they could be seen to do the right thing.

> After Tania died, her sister, Miriam, told me that she was "smiling inside but my face is very sad outside". When I asked what stopped her smiles from showing outside, she explained to me "everybody must be sad now so they can see we can miss Tania . . . so then, how can mama know—I can't keep telling?"

It seems that there are unspoken rules that govern our expression of feeling from an early age when we learn to enact an "emotional role". We learn that certain situations call for particular emotional expressions, and we might feel morally inferior if expected emotions are not genuinely experienced. In this way emotions confirm societal values and involve the moral order; as cultural practices and theories they are constructed in interaction with and with reference to the evaluation of others. Above, Miriam is showing us how, in response to her sister's death, she begins to construct her sadness emotion in relationship with her mother and with reference to the evaluation of "everybody" and "they", referring to her extended family and their community in Peru. Weeks later she told me that the priest had told her that she should be happy that Tania was with God and the angels. By including the priest, God, and the angels with her audience, Miriam began to open opportunities for a wider repertoire of emotional expression.

Emotions commonly associated with death or bereavement include numbness, shock, anger, guilt, sadness, and despair and are reflected in the normative theories of death and mourning that we have addressed in this chapter. As Miriam has shown us, to associate love, enthusiasm, or creativity with the early stages of the grieving process is commonly considered inappropriate or even pathological or bizarre. Normative theories of grief are most commonly used by professionals in hospitals to guide their practice and have usually been constructed within the context of dominant cultural and religious beliefs. The normal emotions associated with grieving in these theories generally relate to a timely, anticipated death that occurs in usual circumstances. The death of a child or young parent is not a usual circumstance, nor is the culture of the hospital.

Eight-year-old Abdul's father had died in a road traffic accident. Abdul was told of his father's death whilst still in hospital for treatment of the injuries sustained in the same accident. Sister Alison, in charge of the ward, asked me to see Abdul to help with "his anger". He was refusing to eat and, formerly a jolly child with a sharp sense of humour, had not spoken for two days. I met with Abdul and his mother on the ward. Abdul was sitting in bed, silently staring at the bedclothes. He refused all my rather awkward invitations to join me in talking.

Glenda: Mrs P [Abdul's mother], now do you understand that Abdul is not talking? What ideas do you have about this?

Mrs P: Abdul is angry—that's why he's silent.

(*I thought I noticed Abdul grimacing, squinting his eyes and raising his shoulders in response to the word "angry".*)

Glenda: Mrs P, how do you understand Abdul is angry?

Mrs P: Sorry?

Glenda: What helps you to know that he is angry?

Mrs P: Sister Alison said so.

Glenda: And what ideas is Sister Alison using to help her know?

Mrs P: I don't know, I didn't ask her.

Glenda: Abdul, do you think you feel angry?

Abdul: (*remains silent*)

(*I thought I saw him grimace or wince as he looked away.*)

Glenda: What is angry? . . . What does an angry person do?

Abdul: (*relaxing his shoulders, looking at the bedclothes*) Mr Angry.

Finding herself in a new and unfamiliar situation, without opportunity to refer to friends, family, or members of her culture and community, Mrs P was unsure how to make sense of Abdul's behaviour. She had no personal experience of losing a parent or of hospitalization in childhood and therefore referred to Sister Alison's authority to help her construct a theory to explain Abdul's silence.

In this way, we are looking at emotions as the theories that people construct to make sense of behaviour and bodily responses. Such constructions are often built on common-sense or cultural-sense, understandings of how people behave; they may draw from memories and knowledges of similar past episodes and are generally evaluated with reference to others. Sister Alison used normative and professional theories of mourning to construct Abdul's emotion as anger, thereby trying to help Mrs P put meaning to his silence. Abdul, however, chose not to accept the meaning offered by his mother and his nurse.

I have frequently encountered children, like Abdul, who refuse the emotions that adults construct for them to explain their behaviour. I have noticed that meanings or descriptions are most commonly refused when a person's sense of worthiness or autonomy seems to be invalidated or when the power of others leads to acknowledgement of his or her own incompetence. Abdul's grimaces and wincing in response to his mother's description of his anger, his own reference to "Mr Angry", and the negative connotations ascribed to anger in children's story books (e.g. Hargreaves, 1978) led me to consider that he may have perceived this self-description, "angry", as a criticism or comment on his incompetence.

We construct emotional theories about people's behaviour and bodily responses in order to inform ourselves or others about how to act. Abdul's mother wanted to understand the meaning of his silence so that she could know how to go on with him: what she might say, how she might help, whether she should be sympathetic, angry, matter-of-fact. We might say, therefore, that a useful theory of emotion is one that opens space for a repertoire of alternative options for action, or creates opportunities for different ways of being, or reminds one of emotional possibilities that may have been disowned or forgotten, and in this process offers freedom and power. Were I to have that conversation with Abdul and his mother now, I would be interested to ask them and Sister Alison:

— If you choose to see Abdul's silence as anger, how does it affect

    . . . how you see/think about/feel about him/yourself?

. . . things between you?

. . . what you might do next/how you are with him?

— How does seeing Abdul as angry help you/him/the hospital?

— If Abdul is helped to think of himself as angry,

. . . what opportunities does it provide?

. . . are there ways that this description gets in the way of things or creates difficulties for you/Abdul?

I would also be interested to explore what alternative emotions for Abdul they might construct, and the associated consequences for meaning, relationships, and action of different emotion constructions. For example:

— If you chose another feeling for Abdul instead of anger, what might you choose?

— What feeling do you think Abdul would like to choose for himself?

— What effect would (this description) have on (relationships, actions, and views of self and others)?

Mr and Mrs M, below, were also looking for some idea about the meaning of their son Jamie's behaviour in order to help them know how to go on with him.

> Ten-year-old Jamie M (Chapter Two) had been treated for leukaemia since he was 6. For the past four years, following a bone-marrow transplant, he had been well. There was recent evidence that the leukaemia had returned. Jamie's parents had been told that the medical team could no longer overcome the leukaemia and that their treatment could continue to ensure only that Jamie was comfortable. Mr and Mrs M had explained this to Jamie.

> The nurses were concerned that Jamie hardly responded to them. They thought that he was withdrawn and depressed and wanted to know what to do. Mr and Mrs M shared the nurses' concerns. They worried that he was not telling them how he was feeling, and they

did not know what to do. They feared that he had given up and doubted whether they should have been so open with him. I met with Jamie, his mother, and his father.

Mrs M: I think Jamie is unhappy but it's hard to know how he really feels because he won't say anything.

Glenda: What are your ideas about how Jamie feels, Mr M?

Mr M: He's not talking to me either—I don't know what to do, much the same as my wife.

Glenda: Jamie, your mum thinks you may be unhappy, your dad says he doesn't know how things are for you at the moment. What do you think about their worries?

Jamie: (shrugs)

Glenda: Jamie, do you feel troubled at all?

Jamie: (shrugs)

Glenda: If you did feel something, how big would this feeling be? Could you show me?

Jamie: (lifts his hand indicating a gap)

Glenda: Could we measure it?

Jamie agreed and, using a tape-measure, I noted that the space between his hands measured fourteen inches. I asked Jamie if he would like to make a model of this feeling, since I knew that he liked modelling with clay. We agreed that Jamie would construct his feeling and that we would meet again. As I left I said maybe he would like to include his dad and mum somehow.

When I saw Jamie again his father was present (parents tended to visit in shifts to share keeping the rest of the family life going). A model about six inches in diameter was sitting next to his bed. I asked his father, "Is this Jamie's feeling?" Mr M said he had watched Jamie construct it and had helped to hold the string: it resembled a solid rectangle with branches, which were connected by a sort of web of strings. Jamie had painted it blue, black, and gold.

Glenda: Does this feeling have a name?

Jamie: (*shakes his head*)

Glenda: If it did have a name, what would you call it?

Jamie: (*rolls his tongue against his top palate and lips, making a sound something like "balup-balup"*)

(*Mr M laughed. Jamie grinned.*)

Glenda: Is balup-balup around you at the moment, Jamie?

Jamie: (*nods*)

Glenda: Do you like feeling balup-balup?

(*Again Jamie shrugged.*)

Glenda: Do you want to keep balup-balup, get rid of it, shrink it, grow it, or something else?

Jamie: Control it.

Glenda: Is balup-balup troubling you now, or do you have it under control?

Jamie: (*looking at the model and then at his father*) Today I'm the controller.

Glenda: I see . . . so what helps you to control balup-balup?

Jamie: When Dad is here.

Glenda: Mr M, how do you help Jamie control balup-balup?

Mr M: (*smiling*) I have no idea, no idea.

Jamie: Tells me I can do things.

I asked Jamie and Mr M if they could take careful notice of the times when balup-balup was out of control, what happened, what and who helped to put it in its place. I suggested that they may want to share this with Mrs M, and maybe the nurses or doctors had a few ideas as well.

I had further meetings with Jamie and his parents when we discussed various plans and strategies that they had employed to deal with balup-balup. Jamie had noticed that treating it kindly helped, and he had added a few painted bolts to cheer it up. Balup-balup changed shape and form over time; Mr and Mrs M, the nurses, doctors, and I also added bits to balup-balup, always in consultation with Jamie. Most of the time that we spoke of balup-balup I was left thinking: "What are we talking about here?" However, for Jamie, his parents, and the nurses the issue never seemed to arise again.

Some weeks later I was walking down the ward when a nurse called me into the staff room—three nurses were waiting expectantly. She said, "Glenda, we're feeling balup-balup, what can we do?" Again, my first thought was: what are we talking about here?

Nursing and medical staff agreed to help me abstract the following key principles that had emerged from our work with children like Jamie and Abdul and might guide our future practice with other children and their families facing similar challenges:

- Attend to use of language

- Join the child's language

- Acknowledge the child's and family's expertise

- Construct a language and theory of emotions in relationship with the child and significant others

- Move away from emotions as self-descriptions

Attend to use of language

Initially I had invited Jamie to use our adult language to describe his feelings: I put forward his mother's description of "unhappy" and then added two other options, "worries" and "troubled". Jamie, however, refused all my descriptions, and the ward staff and I recounted, between us, numerous other examples where children, like Jamie and Abdul, had refused our descriptions of their feelings. In the majority of situations, our uses of words like "cross", "jealous", or "scared" had created an impasse in our work with the child.

We reflected on our tendency to use adult language when talking with children about feelings and emotions. We recognized that we commonly altered words to reflect what we *thought* sounded like child talk—for example, "scary" for afraid, or "cross" for angry—but that, essentially, *we* usually introduced the emotional construct ourselves and, in large part, were coming from our adult perspective and expectations of children's feelings.

Join the child's language

Rather than seeing children's refusal of our descriptions of their feelings as their denial or repression, we chose to focus on *our* difficulty with joining their grammar (Cronen & Lang, 1994) and opening space for preferred actions and positive sense of selves.

Noting that Jamie was communicating non-verbally, I asked him to *show* me (rather than tell me) the size of his feeling and in this way joined his grammar—the rules he was using—by responding to his *showing* with my own actions (measuring his feeling). Continuing to coordinate (Pearce, 1994) with Jamie's grammar, I suggested that he make his feeling through modelling clay, a non-verbal medium of his preference.

Acknowledge the child's and family's expertise

We were willing to hand over authority to Jamie and acknowledge that he was the expert on his feeling. In this way we resisted the temptation to colonize his language and that of his parents with the use of professional discourse.

Eliciting this principle evoked a very interesting discussion when a trainee psychologist challenged us by asking what effect joining the child's language would have on our credibility with the medical profession—did we not need to demonstrate that we could engage in medical discourse? I return to this dilemma in Chapter Six.

Construct a language and theory of emotions
in relationship with the child and significant others

Following Jamie's authority, we used a new shared language to construct a conjoint theory of his emotion. We encouraged Jamie to include his family in the construction, and, with his permission, we joined this process as soon as was acceptable to him and his parents. In this way we worked towards constructing Jamie's feeling in relationship with his parents and most of the ward staff.

I invited Jamie to name his feeling giving him the authority, and instead of receiving "balup-balup" as nonsense we embraced it in pursuit of its meaning and uses. If language is approached as a form of action rather than a form of representation, it follows that meanings and understandings will emerge and change in the course of inter-actions. It is therefore not necessary to ensure that all persons have exactly the same understanding of the utterance or symbol; what is necessary is that they develop abilities to coordinate their language and actions with each other in ways that make sense and allow them to go on (Cronen & Lang, 1994). In this way Jamie, his parents, and significant nurses and doctors mutually coordinated in relation to balup-balup without "knowing" the representational meaning of the word.

An utterance is only non-sense when we do not know how to go on to use it in a sensible or coherent way. To know the meaning of a word, then, is to know how to use it and how to respond to it in a particular context (Wittgenstein, 1953). Balup-balup, therefore, challenged us to refer continually to Jamie's expertise on its uses and how best to respond to it. In this way we were encouraged to ask Jamie questions like:

— What is balup-balup up to today? How is it making things for you at the moment?

— Do you want it to be that way, or would you like it to be different?

— Is balup-balup any good for anyone at the moment? Who is most pleased with the way it is? How is balup-balup making things between you and your mum at the moment?

— What would you like to do for/with balup-balup now? Who would you like to help you with this?

— What will happen if we do ____ to balup-balup? How will it affect things for you and your dad?

In this way the meaning of balup-balup emerged in its use, and we needed to attend constantly to Jamie's context without making assumptions.

Move away from emotions as self-descriptions

Sister Alison and Mrs P asked me to help Abdul with *his* anger in order to ensure that he would talk again, and the medical team wanted me to cure Jamie of *his* depression.

It is not uncommon for professionals or parents to construct with each other emotions like these, on behalf of children and without their participation in the process. Frequently the emotion is further redefined as "a problem" and identified as internal to the child. Significant family members and professionals are commonly affected by such "problems" and, in situations like this, may then call in an "expert" to take the problem away.

When Mrs P and Sister Alison suggested "Abdul is angry", he may have experienced himself as "Mr Angry" and the description as attributing anger to *his* identity and ascribing to himself certain (angry) traits and (angry) ways of being. To avoid involving Abdul in such a process of negative self-description, I could have asked him what Mr Angry did and how Mr Angry was affecting him and his mother. In this way I could have invited Abdul to externalize the emotion—anger—instead of approaching it as internal to himself (White, 1989a).

Externalizing, here, involves encouraging the child and significant others to objectify, or at times personify, emotions or feelings that are experienced as undermining or overwhelming (Epston, 1992). Jamie M and his parents were invited to externalize his feeling when Jamie was asked to make a model of it. In this way we moved away from seeing the feeling as the child per se, as internal to the child, or as belonging to the child: balup-balup did not become a trait or characteristic (*Jamie is balup-balup*), nor did we attribute balup-balup to a property of his sole ownership (*Jamie has balup-balup*). By asking Jamie to make his feeling and then to name it, he was invited to position this feeling outside himself so that it became a separate entity. This enabled a new relationship with the emotion, thereby enhancing personal agency and opening more opportunity for action for Jamie and his carers. If Jamie had become balup-balup (*Jamie is balup-balup*), he would have been required to control himself should he have wanted to keep the feeling under control. By being helped to separate himself and his relationships from the emotion through the process of externalization, Jamie was able to involve other family members and staff in this task; the process of externalization therefore opened up the possibility for them to support each other in the control of balup-balup (White, 1991).

* * *

A colleague asked me whether I thought he should go in to work on his day off to sit with a family whose daughter was dying. He explained that they were alone in this country, having recently arrived from abroad for special treatment for their child. I asked what ideas, theories, or experiences would inform his decision to go in and his decision to take the day off. He replied, "Human theories—I believe it is the human thing to do."

Dealing with death can pose anxiety and confusion for professionals with clients, for family members with each other, and for parents with children. Theories can offer guidance, clarity, and the security of a way to proceed. They can also offer a distance from the experience. In order to manage the anxiety and confusion that death can pose, some of the people in this chapter have risked ritualizing the few psychological theories of experts in the field, turning them into policy and procedures for "good practice" on how to die and how to deal with death and dying. In our attempts to adapt death and dying to the language of technology and efficiency, we risk evolving a language that is incompatible with enabling people to come to terms with the existential crises that death presents and to go on living. Having reviewed some of the personal and professional theories and beliefs about death (Chapter Two) and mourning (this chapter), I move on in Chapters Four and Five to discuss how clients and professionals might be helped to identify, appraise, and create *their* preferred theories of death and grieving to guide their choice of actions.

CHAPTER FOUR

Creating new stories

Alan described how he and his children would make up stories together at bedtime. Recently, 4-year-old Ron had been "introducing death into the stories"; 2-year-old Sarah "would always add a princess or two". Alan acknowledged with amusement his attempts to "sugar the pill". Each time Ron "killed off a character", Alan would find more inventive ways of bringing that person back to life with "reviving drinks, reversal spells—you name it" .

In order to make sense of our lives, we organize our experiences of events, thoughts, and feelings into coherent accounts in a way that such narratives can give meaning to our experiences. These stories can create for us a sense of continuity in our lives and provide a framework for interpreting further experiences. Therefore we live our lives according to those stories that we tell ourselves and those that we are told by others. Our stories shape our lives, influencing which experiences we pay attention to, give meaning to, and continue to incorporate into our constantly evolving narratives (White & Epston, 1990).

We construct our stories in relationship with others, including our families, cultures, and religions. In the absence of one dominant story about death, people may draw on many traditions to construct their preferred stories to guide their meanings and actions. Above we see how Alan and his children, Ron and Sarah, begin to construct their shared story about death. Four-year-old Ron, who has no direct experience of death, may be trying to make sense of the notion by incorporating it into the stories he creates with his father and sister. In time, Alan, Ron, and Sarah may come to a synthesis of their different contributions.

Over time much of our lived experience goes unstoried and hence is never "told" or expressed. Although everyone has to anticipate the future death of parents, friends, and parts of themselves, many parents tell me that they have never explained death to themselves, and several participants on courses I have run report that they have never worked out a coherent account for themselves of what happens after a person dies.

> Alan told me that he and his partner were "fortunate that neither of us has experienced a close death". He had never contemplated his parents' deaths, and Ron and Sarah had come no closer to death than through stories and films. He noted how his contributions to the story that they were creating together reflected several tales created by adults for children in which dead grandmothers miraculously come back to life, unconscious princesses are awakened by the kiss of a prince, old men are revived after one hundred years of sleep, and small mice flattened against walls recover fully to resume action.

Having to explain death to children therefore challenges the adult to make overt ideas and beliefs that she or he may never before have had to articulate. Children's questions may invite adults overtly to construct their own stories about death for the first time. People may therefore seek guidance from professionals for developing a death story that makes sense for themselves and their children.

Exploring death stories with families

Mrs T (Chapter One) wanted to know how she could explain death to her 9-year-old twin boys Daniel and Benjamin, whose father had died suddenly and unexpectedly five months previously. Since her husband's death, she had been following the advice of her counsellor, which had helped her to respect the boys' own thoughts and feelings as well as normalize the distress that they had witnessed others expressing. She had also focused on enabling them to feel important and encouraging them to continue with their age-appropriate activities. However she had "come unstuck" when contemplating how to explain death to the children in a way that she thought might make sense to them, and invited me to give her my professional view about what to say.

When parents ask for help with talking to their children about death, I usually respond to their request by first **exploring the beliefs and stories about death** in the family. I therefore asked Mrs T, Daniel, and Benjamin:

— How do you explain death to yourself? Which ideas about death are you most comfortable with?

— What do you believe (happens when people die/after people die)?

I ask all family members for their views and enquire about the beliefs and stories of other significant people who are not present at our meeting. In this way I explore the death stories from the point of view of the child, the parents and other family members, their community, and the professionals or agencies involved with the family. I try to avoid dichotomies of agree–disagree by asking questions such as:

— Is that the way you think about it, or do you have a different idea (from your brother)?

— What different thoughts do you have about it?

— What would others say in your community/family?

In response to questions about their ideas on death, Benjamin T replied only that he did not know. Daniel said he could hear his father's voice at night but did not know where he was and answered my questions with several questions of his own, including who would be keeping his father company and whether he was in pain. Mrs T told me she was attending spiritualist meetings, that her family did not approve, and that she was unsure whether she "believed". She repeated several times "If I don't know myself—how can I tell the boys?"

In the course of a conversation like this, I might address the family's ideas about what they think they can "know" and what they think they can "believe" by asking such questions as:

— What can you know about . . . ? How can you know it?

— (If you cannot know) what would you like to believe?

— What helps you to believe that? What stops you believing in this way/what interferes with that belief?

In this way I would be trying to **generate an ecology of ideas and stories about death** (Bateson, 1972), which the family and I might use as a resource from which to construct a new story that fits for each of them and gives suitable meaning to their experience. I therefore encourage people to tap into their many and varied sources of stories about death, both past and current, and to take different lenses or perspectives—for example, those of religion, gender, or culture. I may therefore ask:

— What are the stories from your religion?

— How are these the same/or different from your cultural beliefs?

— If you were a man/woman, how might you think of it?

Thus I invite family members to entertain multiple and possibly contradictory ways of thinking about death. In my response to their ideas and stories I try to avoid an evaluative stance that might suggest that the views can be right or wrong, good or bad. I take a deliberate "not-knowing" position (Anderson & Goolishian, 1992), reflecting and inviting the family to "play" with a variety of different perspectives. In this way, I try early on with the family to set a context that we will not be thinking about death explanations as objective or intrinsic truths, but rather as ideas or stories that may or may not be afforded truth status.

When people tell me that they do not know what they believe, I sometimes invite them to "do some research" and to ask other people in their family or community to share their stories of death. I suggest that they bring the ideas back to our next meeting so that we can pool all the ideas and go on to talk together about those that they like and those that do not fit.

> Daniel took the "research" task very seriously and asked several pupils at school to tell him what happens when someone dies. This initially created a degree of concern amongst teaching staff, who received a couple of 'phone calls from parents wanting explanations for their children's sudden preoccupation with death. It also prompted Daniel and Benjamin's teacher to conduct a special lesson on death with their class.

Sometimes I offer a selection of children's stories about death as a potential source of alternative ideas that the family might integrate into their evolving death narrative. Occasionally I relate my version of the story or lend children's books to the family to read together and review so that we can discuss what they like and do not like about the stories and what bits of which stories fit with their other preferred ideas. In Chapter Six I present an approach to using children's stories to co-create meaningful narratives about death with families. A selection of books written for children about death is provided in Appendix B.

Coordinating stories

The stories we privilege evolve over time. They may be drawn from cultural, religious, or professional contexts and do not always fit with current personal circumstances. People may approach a therapist for help with creating new or alternative narratives when the story they are telling themselves does not fit with their lived circumstances, thus leaving them feeling unhappy or disconnected. Privileged stories about death and mourning commonly have evolved in relation to a timely or expected death—for example, the death of an elderly relative—and may jar with the experience of the death of a child.

> Shortly after the death of her son Georgie, Ms H (Chapter One) was visited by the vicar, who told her that little Georgie was at peace with God. Ms H was furious. She did not want Georgie to be with God at all, she wanted him with her at home. "And if he has to be with God, it hurts to think he is happy and at peace there, away from his mummy." Georgie had died at the age of 6, far too soon for such a sudden separation. He had started school three months before his death, having endured a long illness for nearly three years. Ms H wanted Georgie to miss her, to need her, to be with her.

Since stories may need to change to accommodate different contexts or new experiences, I may invite clients and professionals to **explore the fit of old or current stories with changing contexts** by asking questions like:

— What ideas (about death) did you have then?/How did you explain (death) to yourself/make sense of it?

— What happens if you use those ideas to make sense of (this situation)?

— How do you understand that (that story) no longer fits/is no longer useful?

Although Ms H had found the vicar's view about death consoling when her father died eight years previously, the same story caused her considerable distress in relation to the death of her son. For Mr L (Chapter One), the explanation that "leukaemia killed" his daughter Monica was sufficient on the day she died. In the months that followed her death, however, he wanted to elaborate his story both to make sense of why she had died so young and to give new meaning to his own existence.

It is through the medium of stories that we create ourselves, each other, and the social worlds in which we live (Pearce, 1994). Therefore we need to construct a narrative about experience which is meaningful and congruous not only for ourselves but also for others with whom we are in significant relationship. Below, Ms H shows how she is trying to find the story through which she and her 3-year-old daughter, Lisa, might create a picture of Georgie and hence the relationship that they can go on to have with him. Ms H has a number of possible theses available to her and is trying to coordinate their fit with her personal experience of the death of her child as well as what she thinks others in her community may believe.

> *Ms H:* Lisa tells me that Georgie is on the moon. Yesterday she asked if Georgie can walk and run. What should I say?
>
> *Glenda:* What do you believe?
>
> *Ms H:* I don't know.
>
> *Glenda:* What would you like to believe?
>
> *Ms H:* That he can dance and skip and sing . . .
>
> *Glenda:* And if you told that to Lisa? How might that make things?
>
> *Ms H:* I think she'd like it really . . . comforting to her . . .
>
> *Glenda:* Any reservations about Lisa thinking this way?
>
> *Ms H:* Not for me . . . but supposing she tells someone else . . . it's sort of like finding out there isn't a Santa Claus . . .
>
> *Glenda:* When did you start believing there isn't a Santa Claus?
>
> *Ms H:* (*laughs*) Isn't there? I can't remember really . . . maybe 6 or 7?
>
> *Glenda:* What effect did that have on you?
>
> *Ms H:* I sort of knew already, in a way . . . it was just something I wanted to believe . . . a sort of comfort.

Ms H begins to create her preferred story about death, and in particular the death of her son Georgie. The story that Georgie is at peace with God does not fit with Ms H's lived experience of the death of her child. The story that Georgie can skip and sing could be comforting and reassuring for her and her daughter Lisa, but when she takes into account Lisa's other potential audiences—such as her friends, teachers, other family members, and members of their community—Ms H begins to re-evaluate this story in the light of how others might react to her preferred ideas. Ms H's doubts about sharing her preferred story with Lisa highlight the difference between telling a story and living it.

Thus Ms H is seeking to construct her preferred narrative, which has a good-enough fit with her lived experience and is meaningful and coherent for herself and 3-year-old Lisa. She is also trying to coordinate the story that they can tell themselves with the stories that they will share in other significant relationships—for example, with family, community, and culture.

Co-constructing preferred stories

After exploring a range of possible views about death with a family, I try to enable a context in which family members might coordinate their preferred theses. Thus we might go on together to construct a narrative that they might tell themselves that makes sense of the death experience for all the family and is coherent with their other stories about life, as well as the stories of others with whom they are in significant relationship.

With the T family below, **I invite each family member to identify their preferred ideas** about death and dying.

> *Glenda:* You have told me so many ideas you have about death. Now could I hear, what are the ideas you like the most? I would like to hear from each of you.

> *Mrs T: (after a few minutes)* I like to think of Graham as always a part of our family—when I did the research you gave us, I asked my cousin, and he said Graham may not be here in body but he'll always be with us in spirit.

> *Glenda:* So your mum likes to think of your dad as with you in spirit. And Benjamin? Which idea do you want to choose?

> *Benjamin: (smiling, shrugs)*

Glenda: You told me your teacher talked to all your class about what happens when people die. Did you learn any ideas you specially liked or did not like?

Benjamin: Caterpillars die when they turn into butterflies.

Glenda: I see . . . do you like that idea? That when someone dies, it's something like what happens when a caterpillar turns into a butterfly?

Benjamin: (*nods*)

Glenda: Is that how you would like to think of your Dad?

Benjamin: (*nods*)

Glenda: Thank you, Benjamin. What about you, Daniel? Have you got a favourite idea you especially like when we are trying to understand your dad's death?

Daniel: Dad tells me what to do. He is always there if I want to ask him something.

Glenda: So, Daniel, you would like to think that you can speak to your dad whenever you want?

Mrs T: (*to Daniel*) You're very lucky. (*To Glenda*) Should I let him carry on like this, or should I stop it? What is your professional opinion?

When people like Mrs T make a point of seeking my *"professional"* opinion, I accept the invitation to **contribute professional theories to the pool of stories** and ideas about death and bereavement that we have been generating with the family. Professional knowledges are commonly privileged above personal and cultural stories. In Chapter One, Sister Lin subjugates her personal knowledges about children and motherhood and privileges her professional story about talking about death. In public services in Britain, people are generally paid to impart their professional stories about death, whereas there is a common expectation that cultural knowledges should be donated by volunteers or kept for personal and not professional relationships. In this way personal knowledges and cultural knowledges are relegated to a lower status in the overall order of knowledges. Moving away from the notion of a hierarchy of knowledges, I try to put forward professional theories not as truths but as more or less useful ideas that might contribute to the creation of the family's preferred stories about death and dying.

Usually I relate, or perhaps narrate, professional theories to families, children, and colleagues, although there have been times when I have shared written material or read out sections of articles. I have noticed how the professional theories that I work with evolve constantly over time in the course of my lived practice and professional development. Therefore the theories that I describe to the T family below are presented neither as truths nor as accurate representations of original theories. Instead they are versions of some of the professional theories that I have gleaned over time and have then co-evolved in conversation with the T family. Each time I relate a theory, it evolves in different ways and is modified in relationship with the audience.

> *Glenda:* I have come across at least three theories that relate to your question. One theory states that a child of about 7 or 8 would have a "mature" understanding of death (Kane, 1979)— so according to this theory most children of Daniel's and Benjamin's age would understand that death is irreversible, that the dead person's body stops working completely and they cannot come alive again. So according to this theory, children who have not reached the stage of a mature concept of death may believe that wishing or doing something special, like magic, might bring the dead person back. If we prefer this theory, then we might see Daniel's talking to his father as showing that he has not yet achieved a mature understanding of death. Or we might think that he wants desperately to bring his father back. What do you think about these ideas? Do they fit for you and Daniel and Benjamin?

> *Mrs T:* Daniel is very intelligent. I'm sure he understands that his father could not really come alive again. Both the boys knew that before they were 6.

> *Glenda:* Your mum says that when you were much younger you understood that a person cannot come alive again after they have died and be exactly the same as they were before they died—is that how you see things now?

> *Daniel:* (*nods*)

Mrs T: But he does miss his father badly . . . I'm sure he would do anything to have him back—maybe he is wishing . . . my counsellor said he cannot accept his father's death.

Glenda: Well, yes. That idea does actually fit with another theory—that those who are left behind after someone has died must be able to say goodbye to that person, to let go of them, to detach themselves so that they can move on in their own lives. How do you find that theory—is it useful for you and the boys?

Mrs T: (*hesitates*) Is it true?

Glenda: These are theories—there is no one-hundred-percent proof. In fact, there is another theory that says the opposite of that one.

Mrs T: (*laughs*)

Glenda: The other theory suggests that children, as well as adults, are able to find different ways of continuing a relationship with people who have died. For example, they may make a connection through visiting the cemetery or speaking to the dead person.

Daniel: We never went to the cemetery.

Mrs T: He means the funeral—their father is buried in Wales. (*To Daniel*) We already told the lady that.

Glenda: Mmm . . . I remember you told me you would have liked to go to your dad's funeral. Well, this theory says there are many different ways of keeping contact, like remembering the dead person or keeping something that belonged to them (Silverman, Nickman, & Worden, 1991). Then there is the idea that people could benefit from sort of saying hello again to someone who has died, especially if they miss them (White, 1989b).

Daniel: (*giggles and nudges Benjamin, who frowns*)

Glenda: There is the idea that when someone is very important in our life they help us to know things about ourselves, for example, to feel good about ourselves or to know that we are important or special. Benjamin and Daniel, what did your father help you to feel good about?

Daniel: Football.

Benjamin: (*grins*)

Glenda: Like they may help us feel proud of something we do, so we can notice how well we play football. So when that person dies, it may feel like that proud part gets lost, as if the proud part dies when that person dies—like we may stop noticing how good we are at football or how much we like football. Am I making any sense?

Mrs T: (*nods, tearfully*) Graham was very proud of his sons.

Glenda: Well, this theory would say that it may help if you included Mr T in your family again, for example, by trying to look at yourselves through his eyes or think about what he would say. The theory would say that this could help bring alive the good and special things he knew, or felt about, or saw in Daniel and Benjamin. In this way it might help the boys (and you) to appreciate themselves through their father's eyes even if he is not here to tell them. I've been chattering on a bit. Could I hear from all of you—we have so many theories now, let's hear who likes what and which ones go well together for your family.

Having elaborated a repertoire of ideas together and identified their preferred stories, the family is invited to **evaluate the different theses** so that they can decide which ones suit them, with questions like:

— Does that fit for you?

— Which bits of that (story) are most important to you?

— Which do you want to keep/put away/get rid of?

— Do you have other ideas that you would like to add?

Reviewing the T family's preferred themes or stories reveals that Mrs T favours the idea that her husband is with the family in spirit. Benjamin chooses the story that portrays death as something like a caterpillar turning into a butterfly, and Daniel contributes that he would like to talk to his father whenever he wants. From the professional theories put forward, Daniel likes the idea of saying hello again to his father, and Mrs T is particularly moved by the idea that the boys have lost their father's contribution to their pride.

Coordinating the family's preferred stories involves **reflection on the fit between their different ideas**. I may therefore invite family members to associate or connect with each other's theses with questions like:

— Mrs T, how does Daniel's wanting to talk to his dad whenever he wants fit with/differ from your idea that their dad is with you all in spirit?

— And how does Benjamin's idea about "death being like a caterpillar becoming a butterfly" fit with/differ from this?

— If we put Daniel's choice of "saying hello again to his dad" together with your choice that "dad is always with you in spirit", what do they have in common, and then what ideas can we come up with?

It may also be useful to explore how the family's evolving narrative relates to other stories and knowledges that they hold; whether new theses that emerge contradict or confirm knowledges from other significant contexts—for example, family, community, religion, or culture. I might therefore ask questions like:

— How are these ideas the same as/different from your religious beliefs?

— What would the Vicar/Rabbi/Imam say if you shared this with him or her?

— Which ideas do your parents prefer? And how do your ideas now fit with theirs?

As well as coordinating the fit of different stories within the family, this approach is intended to enable members to evolve a new story that represents more than just the sum of their individual contributions. Juxtaposing their divergent ideas invites the family to make new connections between their different theses and creates opportunities for new stories to emerge. With the perception of difference, new contexts can evolve, giving new meaning to old ideas (Bateson, 1979).

With the evolving and unfolding of new narratives, I invite people to **address the implications and effects of their stories for individuals and relationships**. I explore how their preferred theses might affect what people do—"If you decide that you will like this (story) best, what are you most likely to do/not do?"—how they feel—"What effect does holding this (story) have on you/your daughter?"—and their views of themselves—"If you choose to think that, how does it affect how you feel about yourself?" I also invite people to consider the implications of certain stories for their relationships—"How does this (story) effect things between you and your parents?/If you shared this with the vicar, what might he or she say/do/think?" In this way I begin to contemplate with the family the possible contexts that a new story might create and hence those opportunities for lived experience made possible for the future.

> Abdul P and his mother (Chapter Three) agreed that everything was God's will, including the death of Mr P. This narrative reassured Mrs P, helping her to feel that there was a good reason for her husband's death. Abdul reported that since everything was Allah's will, Allah must have wanted his father to die. This made him think that since Allah is good, he, Abdul, must have done something wrong to make Allah cross. The effect of this narrative on Abdul brought forth "bad" feelings "inside" and the belief that he was a "bad" boy.
>
> Abdul's story overwhelmed me, so that, like Abdul, I was unclear how I could proceed in any way that could be of help to him. If I joined him in his story, I would be confirming that he was a "bad" boy; however, if I disagreed with his views, I would be undermining his religious beliefs and negating the story that was helping him and his family to make sense of his father's death. Since a medical colleague commented with concern about my posture when he saw me stooped, contemplating this dilemma outside Abdul's cubicle, I shared my predicament with him. In

turn he shared his experience that "there is always an exception if you look for it ... I learnt this when I was doing my house job which involved a lot of genetic counselling ... as a Catholic it helped me ... just ask them and you'll find the contradictory rule".

Since I am not versed in Moslem theses I took my colleague's advice and invited Abdul and his mother to explore alternative theses to Abdul's privileged story. When I asked Mrs P, "Is there another way you might understand Allah's will here?", without hesitation she said that this could be "a test". When I asked if it could be possible that Allah chose good people to test, Mrs P confirmed with enthusiasm that Allah could well set such a hard test for only those people who are considered to have the strength and courage to meet it.

My medical colleague was suggesting that I invite the family to identify the exception or anti-thesis that contradicts their privileged thesis. I have found that juxtaposing different theses in this way can be especially useful when people, like Abdul, create preferred stories that produce negating feelings that lead to undermining actions or bring forth disapproving views of self. Inviting exceptions, contradictions, and opposites enables the possibility for people to make new connections and associations between their thesis and the alter-theses, thereby creating opportunities for syntheses that might offer new meanings and alternative options for action. Initially Abdul P's privileged story about his father's death, informed by his Moslem belief that this was *Allah's will*, brought forth a negative view of himself as a *bad* boy whose father's death was a punishment from Allah. When his mother was invited to identify a different thesis from Abdul's "punishment" story, she proposed a "test". The juxtaposing of "test" with "punishment" created new meanings for Mr P's death: still seen as Allah's will, the synthesis emerged as one of a "hard test set for only those boys whom Allah might consider strong and courageous enough to undergo it". Previously undermined by his view of himself as a "bad" boy, the evolution of this new story created opportunities for Abdul to see himself as courageous in his attempt to embrace the challenge of his future.

Translating stories into creative actions

Creating new narratives involves reflecting on the thesis and playing with the alter-theses towards the synthesis and emergence of a
new story. With the evolution of a new narrative, I invite people to
evaluate when and where they might choose to use particular stories. I also **explore the implication of the new story for action,** with
questions like:

— Now you have these ideas, what might you choose to do?

— How will this affect what you do next?

> After the T family had reviewed their preferred stories about death
> in our sessions, Mrs T decided to take the boys to Wales to visit
> their father's grave. On their return they came to see me for their
> final session. Daniel and Benjamin were both full of enthusiasm to
> tell me about their journey and in particular to describe to me
> their "jar". Mrs T explained that, quite spontaneously, the boys
> had collected pieces of grass and some stones and sticks from
> around their father's grave. On returning home they had, without
> prompting, placed these items in a glass jar and set it on a table in
> their bedroom, in front of their mirror. I reflected that the boys
> seemed to be "glowing with pride" as they described this "beauti-
> ful jar". Did Mrs T notice this pride? Did Benjamin feel it? Did
> Daniel enjoy it? After they had all acknowledged their pleasure in
> their pride, I asked whether it was anything like the pride they got
> from Mr T.

During our work together, Mrs T, the twins, and I co-created a
story about the death of Mr T in which key themes emerged. These
included his death in body and continuity in spirit, ways of staying
connected and keeping a sense of his presence alive, and his important contribution to his sons' pride. We had co-evolved a narrative
that could make sense of Mr T's death for all members of the family
and was coherent with the beliefs and stories of their extended
family. However, as yet we had involved ourselves only in the
telling of the story, and although the family left their second session
quite pleased with the work we were doing together, I reflected

with a colleague afterwards on the somewhat sterile quality of our co-evolved narrative.

It was during their visit to Wales that the T family began to live the story they had evolved in therapy, thereby putting life into their new narrative. Through visiting Mr T's grave, creating their "jar", and displaying it as a memorial in the twins' room, they enacted or translated their story into action. Their new actions contributed to developing a coherent ritual and marker that had meaning for all members of the family and, furthermore, could create opportunities for new stories to emerge about their father's death and his involvement in their life. The creation of their own memorial to their father seemed to resolve the boys' wish to attend his funeral and reconnect them with the sense of pride and positive views of themselves that they had previously experienced in their relationships with him.

* * *

The T family and I evolved a story about Mr T's death which they went on to translate into action. The principles that guided our conversations included:

- *Creating a non-evaluative atmosphere*

  Avoiding dichotomies of agree–disagree or right–wrong, I invited the family to take different perspectives—for example, to look at an issue from the perspective of their culture, religion, or gender or to consider their views from the position of another person in their family or community.

- *Generating a repertoire of stories with the family*

  By asking all family members for their views and for the perspectives of significant people who were not present, we could begin to explore the beliefs and stories about death in the family and community. To extend their repertoire of narratives, I suggested that they could also research how others believe and think about death and offered to share a selection of alternative (personal or professional) theses.

- *Constructing preferred stories*

  I asked each family member to evaluate the different stories and to identify their preferred ideas, inviting them to make connections between each other's choices. We went on to explore how their evolving narratives related to other stories and knowledges that they were holding, and to address the implications and effects of their stories for individuals and relationships.

- *Translating stories into actions*

  I asked the family to consider how they might use their new ideas in an attempt to explore the implications of their new story for action.

Experience with the T family shows how stories shape actions, which in turn modify and give new meanings to stories. Work with the T family began at the level of story and beliefs. In Chapter Five I begin the work with people at the level of action. Adapting the same processes and practices as those described above, I show how we attempt to co-evolve actions, including rituals and ceremonies, that make sense of loss and death and are coherent with people's significant relationships and stories.

Creating memories towards "co-memorating"

David (aged 12), Joanna (aged 8), and Martin (aged 5) all sobbed when they spoke of their grandmother's death. Mrs E reported that the family had "not been ourselves since nan died". Mr E reported that he and his wife had attended the cremation, but it had been "pointless—we made nothing of it. Odd to have something where my mum did not take part. She was always part of everything we did in our family—Sunday lunch, birthdays ... David came along, but we could see no point in bringing the little ones—it meant nothing to us. Nothing special—not like she was."

Some people come for help lamenting that they have no ideas at all about what to *do* at times of loss and bereavement and seek a prescribed format to guide their action. For the E family, the actions and events available for mourning at the time of their grandmother's death seemed hollow, lacking the special meanings that they associated with her. Mr E complained that the cremation ceremony disconnected them from a sense of her presence, which he saw as essential to the occasion. Therefore the event offered family members no genuine sense of healing. For others the dilemma is not so much how to act, but rather how to negotiate a way to act within a context that does not open space for their preferred actions.

> Anne lost a much-wanted pregnancy at three months. She told me that "the hardest thing is, nobody knows. And nobody cares. If I had gone on longer, the full pregnancy, I would have lost a baby, then people would have noticed ... the doctor even said, "Maybe it was just as well, maybe there was something wrong there". Anne wept: "This was my baby. So no one else knew [the baby], but I did." She spoke of a "huge aching hole" she was carrying silently and felt it could have helped if someone else had also had a relationship with her baby.

Potential parents who have lost pregnancies, like Anne, have told me how they wished for a formal ritual to create recognition of their loss and space for their mourning. Anne experienced her grief as solitary and unacknowledged. She thought a recognized symbol could make her loss visible to others and thereby mark the death of her unborn child.

> After 7-year-old Tania died, the nurses on the paediatric ward reported that both her mother and her sister, Miriam, seemed "frozen". Although they had seen many people numbed by the shock of the impact of death, the nurses thought that the quality of Miriam's demeanour seemed somewhat different. Mrs V would visit Tania in the Chapel of Rest, while Miriam sat motionless on her own in the hospital play room for large parts of the day, insisting that "Tania cannot be dead until Louis arrives". There was no possibility that her cousin Louis, or any family members, could be present for Tania's burial. Mrs V and her two daughters had recently migrated on their own, and Miriam was reflecting their disconnection from community and family.

Because of cultural disruption due to migration, Mrs V and Miriam were unable to participate in their usual grieving actions, neither mourning rituals nor ceremonies. Prior to her sister's death, Miriam had told me (Chapter Three) that she could not engage in different sorts of "knowing" about Tania's dying without the context of her extended family from Peru.

Unsure how to be, how to act, or who to be in the context of their losses, people may therefore need to go beyond their normative rituals to create special actions, unique metaphors, and different symbols, which might offer options for future action and opportunities for healing. In this chapter I adapt the processes and practices described in Chapter Four towards co-evolving new rituals and ceremonies with people who have experienced loss. Together we explore ways of marking their loss, expressing their grief, and affirming their life and relationships with the deceased that are meaningful and consonant with the values of their family, community, cultures, and religions.

Creating actions to in-form stories

Initially I usually invite people to describe their familiar ways of mourning so that, together, we can **explore a range of mourning practices, including rituals and ceremonies,** with questions like:

— How do you mourn and grieve? (What do you normally do after someone has died?)

— What do you think helps?

— What would your parents/family/community (in Peru) do?

In this way I explore whether clients prefer particular prescribed rituals for managing the dying, the dead body, the disposal of the body, or commemorating the loss. I also invite beliefs about emotional expression and ideas about gender or age "rules" for approaching death; for example, I asked Miriam V:

> *Glenda:* Your papa was a grown-up man, and Tania is a child and a girl—would you want it to be the same as you did when papa died? Or does it make a difference what you do this time— since Tania is a little girl and only 7 years old ?
>
> *Miriam:* Tania will need a very pretty dress.

Glenda: A very pretty dress? So that would be different from what happened with your papa?

Miriam: (*nods*)

Glenda: And anything else?

Miriam: (*smiling*) She could wear some wings like an angel.

Glenda: Uh huh, wings like an angel. Mrs V, do you also see differences between what you did after your husband died and what you might do now —Tania being a child and a girl?

Mrs V: She is a child. She will have a special passage.

I was interested in the V family's own experiences as well as the **views of other significant people** for them, which included family and community who were not present. Having been "introduced" to many members of their family and community through our conversations, I was enabled to ask questions like:

— What would Miriam's teacher be doing if she were here now? And Cousin Louis?

— What would they say to Tania or about Tania?

— Would they give her anything or leave anything by her side?

In this way I worked towards **generating an ecology of ideas and practices for mourning** which the V family and I might use as a resource from which to create new rituals and ceremonies consistent with their current context. Mrs V and Miriam contributed a wealth of experience and knowledges of mourning practices informed by their family and cultural stories as well as by their many participations in death and mourning rituals in their home village in Peru.

I could therefore go on to invite Miriam and Mrs V to **identify their preferred actions, symbols, and ceremonies** and also to **evaluate the different practices** so that they could decide which ones suited them, with questions like:

— Does that fit for you?

— Which bits of that (ceremony/ritual) are most important to you?

— Which do you want to keep/put away/get rid of?

— Do you have other ideas you would like to add?

Miriam and her mother chose immediately to talk about their large family in Peru. Miriam wanted someone available at all times to stay with Tania before the funeral, "like Louis looked after Papa". Mrs V said Miriam kept asking her who could come to the "party" to celebrate Tania's life after the burial.

* * *

When I invited Anne to reflect on the grieving practices that she was familiar with, she described her participation in Jewish mourning rituals following the death of her grandparents. She explained that although she did not see herself as religious in any way, she joined in the rituals as part of her "culture" and, in particular, valued burning a memorial candle and participating in seven days of sitting and talking with family and community, sharing memories and stories about her grandparents. She was unsure how her partner would prefer to mourn and grieve and was interested to ask him.

Since the E family had initially reported that they had no preferred ideas about what to do at times of loss and bereavement, I asked if they would like to hear about some of the ideas and practices that other people have used. Their agreement gave me the opportunity to **contribute alternative practices and knowledges, professional, religious, or cultural,** to their pool of ideas about mourning and grieving. In this sort of situation, I may also invite people to do some "research" into the mourning practices of others.

Mrs V and Miriam were not short of ideas about how they would like to mourn and grieve the death of Tania. Anne, too, identified a repertoire of valued mourning practices for herself, which she drew from her religion and culture. I therefore went on with them to **explore the fit of their old or familiar rituals or ways of mourning with their changing contexts,** by asking questions such as:

— What would happen if you try to do that now/here?

— How do you understand that (that action/symbol) no longer
fits/is no longer useful?

Again Miriam insisted that Tania could not be buried without the
arrival of the family from Peru. Since there was no possibility of
cousin Louis or any other family members being present for
Tania's funeral, I acknowledged the poor fit between the family's
preferred rituals and their current context.

* * *

Anne valued the communal activities of her cultural mourning
rituals but saw these practices as a very poor fit with the circumstances of her miscarriage. Since her loss was not openly recognized or acknowledged, she was suffering a solitary grief and felt
that she could not share her sorrow with family or friends.

Sometimes I **invite clients to represent the voices of available
or absent significant people** in the conversations we have and the
plans we create about ways to go on. I may therefore ask:

— Who else could help (if the family cannot be here from Peru)?

Miriam mentioned their priest, and Mrs V turned to the interpreter,
who nodded. Including the interpreter in our conversation, we
went on to discuss ways that the absent family and community
from Peru could have their presence felt, with questions like:
What special contribution would Louis make if he was here? How
could Miriam feel that Louis was with them in spirit? How could
we create a sense that Tania was not alone in the Chapel of Rest?
Was there any person or any thing that could stand for Louis—
Miriam's former teacher, the family priest from their home town,
Mrs V's mother? What might they do or say?

In this way I attempt to evolve a "sense" of family or community
with clients who recognize that they are missing a context of relationships that could open space for mourning and grieving. From
here we might co-evolve new rituals by **exploring new and alternative (mourning) actions and symbols.**

The interpreter asked whether Mrs V had any photographs of Louis or other family members, and between us there emerged the creating of something like a shrine or gallery of symbols representing absent family and community. Miriam contributed her drawing of "Tania with the angels", and Mrs V wanted a photograph of her late husband included.

* * *

When I asked Anne whom she most wanted to join with in the acknowledgement of her loss, she was able to identify two friends and a colleague as well as her partner, who she thought might be "persuaded". We also discussed whether they might want to involve others, and I wondered whether Anne would like to invite their ideas about the sorts of rituals or ceremonies fitting for the loss of the baby she had been looking forward to. I had in mind that we might coordinate a ceremony with Anne and her identified "community of mourners". After this conversation, Anne cancelled her next two appointments. Contacting me two months later, she told me that she had spent a lot of time talking to people and was astounded to learn how many women had "gone through miscarriages" and had felt the same way that she had about the "conspiracy of silence". She was surprised to learn that her partner had felt "shut out" following their loss, and she now saw herself as fortunate to have had "a physical relationship" with the baby. When I asked whether she had thought about performing a ritual or ceremony with some of the people she had mentioned, Anne replied that she had "already had one in a way".

In the above I have tried to facilitate people's own creativity to invent rituals and evolve ceremonies that might address their needs for healing and for celebration. Although I have highlighted in bold certain guiding principles or practices contributing to this process, it is important to recognize that new rituals to address loss need to be carefully co-created with people, in the contexts of their significant relationships and cultures, and not imposed. When I began working with Anne, I had the idea that we might coordinate a ceremony in the health centre where we were meeting so that she could join with her "community of mourners" to acknowledge the loss of her unborn child. When we met again, I was still in pursuit of this plan, failing to address the new meanings that Anne had given to the interactions and conversations that she had engaged in since our last meeting. With patience, Anne clarified for me that she had *"already had"* her ritual. Thus Anne reminded me of the need continually to **reflect on the meanings of actions and symbols for individuals and relationships** and to take care to **leave aspects of rituals unplanned** so that they can evolve and merge to fit the contexts of time, place, and relationships at the moment that they are enacted. My conversations with Anne may have sown the seeds for her involving family, friends, and colleagues in different sorts of interactions about miscarriage and the loss of her expected child. By taking these conversations and ideas about her loss beyond the health centre, she could evolve a ritual to embrace her personal meanings, which perhaps connected her with her culture and family through actions akin to the collective talking and sharing that she valued after the death of her grandparents.

Creating new rituals involves identifying symbols and metaphorical actions that fit for the individual and his or her family, community, religion, age, gender, and culture. Such symbols can enable those involved to relate to multiple meanings in the ritual, and the actions offer opportunity for expression beyond the verbal domain (Imber-Black, 1991). Through the co-creation of their "shrine", which incorporated symbols reflecting their cultural and family traditions, Mrs V and Miriam simultaneously connected with their past and also created something new to acknowledge the changes in their present. In this way their ritual could both connect them with the familiar and provide a transition towards the new and the unknown, thereby creating opportunities for their future. Hence rituals are able to embrace several contradictions simultaneously; this makes them fit well with the process of mourning, which might involve grieving and celebrating as well as moving on.

Co-creating a memory towards co-memorating

Since Mr E's mother had participated in so many aspects of their family's lives, he could not imagine "making something" of an event, like the cremation, where their nan did not take part. For any action or event to have a "point", nan's presence would need to be included in a way that acknowledged her death and was consistent with her "special" meaning to all members of the family.

Early on in our conversation, therefore, I attempted to bring forth memories that family members valued and wanted to hold onto in relation to their nan. I had the idea that through a process of sharing memories and elaborating their current meanings, we could find ways of connecting the family's past with nan to their present, so that new possibilities might be opened for the future. However, I noticed that the family seemed to disengage from our conversation when I asked questions like "I didn't know your nan, could you tell me about her?" "What do you remember about your nan?" "When you think of her, what comes to mind?" "What do you miss most now that nan has died?"

> Mr and Mrs E said very little in response to these questions. The children did share some of their memories of nan; however, their answers were somewhat stilted and their recollections brief and essentially material. Martin, for example, said that "she had brown hair", Joanna reported that "she liked Rich Tea biscuits", and David added that "she lived in a flat".

It was difficult to elaborate new meanings from the children's recollections since their reports seemed sterile and disconnected from their relationships with nan and from their family contexts. However, when I moved on to ask the family "How do you remember nan?", the parents and the children showed more enthusiasm, and a different sort of conversation ensued.

> *David:* At night I find the brightest star that shines and I look at it.
>
> *Glenda:* So looking at the brightest star helps you remember nan—keeps her clear in your mind?
>
> *David:* (*nods*)
>
> *Martin:* We sniff Joanna's dog.
>
> (*Joanna and Martin giggle.*)
>
> *Glenda:* Sniff her dog? I don't understand. What kind of dog have you got, Joanna?

Martin: (*giggling*) No it's a toy—it's blue. Joanna sprayed it with the perfume from nan's dressing table.

Glenda: So it smells like nan? So the dog helps you remember nan, how she smelled? Does her smell sort of bring her closer to you?

Martin: (*grinning, nods*)

Glenda: How does she smell?

Joanna: It's that perfume with the butterfly on the bottle.

Glenda: I see. So is that the way you choose to remember nan, Joanna, by holding on to her smell?

Joanna: I've got all the things she made me—and the picture of her.

Mr E: I had copies made of the last photo we took of her. Enlarged it. Gave one to my brother and the others in the family. A good likeness.

Joanna: We've got ours in a frame.

Martin: Flowers on it.

Mr E: On the table, isn't it? With the dog (*smiling at Martin*) and a few things David picked up from her flat.

In retrospect, I suspect that the *"what"* memory questions that I asked earlier on in the conversation may have urged the E family to objectify their nan, through separating their memories of her from their relationships and experiences with her, thereby setting her apart from the family in just the way Mr E did not want. The family may therefore have experienced my *"what"* memory questions as a coercion towards placing their (memory of) nan outside the family at a time when they were trying to find ways of confirming her presence within the family. *"What"* memory questions invite people to **"re-collect"** or **"re-call"** events, episodes, or images and therefore reflect a model of memory as the fixed and stable property of individuals, held in their heads. *"How"* questions, on the other hand, invite people to connect themselves in relationship through the action of **re-membering**. *"How"* questions therefore reflect a model of memory as extending beyond the individual skin to incorporate relationships. In response to the *"How"* questions above, the E family began to transform their lifeless memories from their past into living memories through the process of re-membering in the present. Hence they opened space for me to explore the family's special meanings of nan by addressing her involvement in their life.

Glenda: What else did nan take part in with you?

Joanna: Holidays.

Martin: We went to Bournemouth.

Mr E: No, that was Brighton—you weren't born when we went to Bournemouth.

Glenda: Did you share times with nan, Mrs E?

Mrs E: She came shopping with me most days, and Christmas of course—every Christmas.

Glenda: Did she make the dinner?

Mr and Mrs E: (*laughing and looking knowingly at each other*)

Mr E: Not quite—well, let's say she commented.

Mrs E: Yes . . . commented (*smiling at Mr E*).

Glenda: So nan was very much a part of all your lives?

Mr E: She had the children after school every day.

Joanna: She took us to the park.

David: I went to her flat.

Mr E: David used to spend a lot of time round her place. They were specially close, him and her—being the first-born and all, you know.

Martin: We fed the ducks.

Joanna: You never came with to the park.

Martin: I did—we sat on the bench.

Joanna: You didn't come feed the ducks.

Mr E: Martin went with nan to the park, too.

Joanna: Not the ducks.

Martin: The bench . . . the sand-pit.

Mr E: Nan took you both to the sand-pit, maybe not the ducks.

Mrs E: I think he did go once.

Martin: And Bournemouth.

David: You weren't born then.

Mr E: You enjoyed that holiday in Brighton. We have a picture of you and Joanna.

Martin: With nan.

Mr E: Well . . . she may have taken the photo.

Here the E family is coordinating memories involving nan that they could take into the future. This **co-memorating** involves much more than simply the pooling of memories and experiences and extends beyond the sum of individuals' perspectives and contributions. The E family is involved in a careful process of deliberation in which they share their various versions of the past, offer varieties of interpretations, and negotiate meanings through a process of joint debate and persuasion.

Initially it is Joanna who sets the context of "holidays with nan" to be re-membered, while Martin quickly follows suit with a memory of a holiday in Bournemouth. It is unclear to me how it came to be that Martin constructed the memory that he was on holiday with the family and nan in Bournemouth, but Mr E immediately contests that memory, correcting Martin with "No, that was Brighton—you weren't born when we went to Bournemouth". When, later on in the conversation, Martin tries once more to make a bid for his inclusion in the family memory of the Bournemouth holiday, David reinforces his father's view that Martin will not be included in that memory, and a shift is made towards incorporating the Brighton experience into the construction of the family's new narrative. Through parents' directions, therefore, certain memories are given voice and hence incorporated into the family's communal memory, whereas others, muted or untold, do not emerge as part of the family's "reality". Thus the E family co-created a memorable story, including nan and a holiday in Brighton, whereas nan's "commenting" was not permitted to become a story told and therefore could not emerge in this episode of co-memorating.

I never found out if nan actually went to Brighton with the family and whether or not it was she who took the photo. For Mr and Mrs E, David, Joanna, and Martin, confirmation of those details seemed immaterial as they continued to construct a shared memory of holidays with nan that included all members of the family. At our next meeting they showed the "memory book" they had created together, entitled "Our Nan", which included the photograph of Brighton and other selected contributions from each member of the family. Whereas the cremation ceremony had disconnected the E family from each other and from their sense of nan, co-memorating enabled them to connect with each other in their remembering of nan's special contributions to their family life.

This process of joint recollecting and reconstructing the past not only influences what the family remembers but also teaches the children something about the process of re-membering (Middleton & Edwards, 1990). By participating in the co-creation of memorable stories of nan, David, Joanna, and Martin are discovering how their memories can become a shared family possession. They are also learning that co-memorating the past involves a process of constant revisions, reconstructions, and selections, as well as negotiations, so that certain memories are confirmed and integrated into their new narrative while others are excluded or modified.

Co-memorating with staff groups

I introduced co-memorating to the practice of a team working with children with life-threatening illness after several unsuccessful attempts to set up staff "support groups" at their request.

> I had been asked by senior nursing staff to provide "support groups" to address the needs of staff involved with the care of children who had died. Despite considerable efforts to accommodate to the constraints of their shifts and demands of their duties, the groups were very poorly attended. Often I found myself meeting only with staff who had never seen the recently deceased child, and frequently student nurses, new on placement, were instructed to attend the groups, with no explanation about the purpose of the meeting. When I reflected with the nurses that this

sort of meeting did not seem to be what people were wanting, they told me that they could see no purpose in "going over the death again". They explained that "we have to get on with our jobs", "we can't dwell on things when we have other children to look after", "it is not going to help them if we're crying big tears all over the place", "it's bad enough going through it at the time— why rake it up again when you're already feeling better". When I asked if it would make a difference if we did not create any space to talk about the dead child, the nurses agreed that they would miss sharing memories of the child. From here we moved towards arranging a trial run of "co-memorating meetings", a space where we could re-member together, sharing stories and thoughts about the deceased children as we knew them.

The co-memorating meetings were open to anyone who wanted to attend. At no time was attendance compulsory or necessary. We made a particular effort to invite carers from the community or other hospitals or units who had been involved with the child who had died on our unit.

One person was asked to convene or facilitate the meeting, which involved managing time and space to talk. Staff teams commonly seem to prefer a facilitator who has not been closely involved with the child. For example, a psychologist from a different unit asked me to convene a co-memoration for a child with whom she had worked closely for two years, so "I can participate for myself".

Over time we evolved a sort of ritual to the meetings, which I have since used to guide co-memorating meetings with other staff groups:

- We would begin with **introductions**, including our **names and a description of each person's involvement with the child** who had died.

- The facilitator would enquire about **connections** between people in the room and their relationship to the child with questions like:

  — Who met Dina first? And how did you become involved?

  — And then who got to know her? Did you meet each other at that time?

These sorts of questions create opportunities for the child's carers to talk about their relationship with each other through their involvement with the child.

> Dina B's physiotherapist mentioned that she would miss working with the play specialist who had helped her "put a bit of fun into some of the more gruelling times", and Dina's nursery teacher said she was pleased to meet Sister Alison, who "figured prominently in all Dina's good news reports".

- **Sharing stories and memories** of the child often leads naturally from the connections that staff make with each other. However, the facilitator might choose to set a context for sharing memories, with a comment like:

  — Does anyone have a story or memory about Dina they would like to share?

- People often spontaneously offer interpretations or different meanings to the stories, and a joint process may evolve of **creating new meanings** in relation to the child and carers.

> When I related that Dina's mother had told me that Dina insisted on steering the hot-air balloon all on her own (Chapter One), one of the nurses added, "that's great, she was ready to go it alone"; another nurse added, "she probably thought her mum could manage without her then"; and the nursery teacher remembered that Dina had insisted her mother have her teddy a few days before she died.

- Ending the meeting usually involves **questions about the future** like:

  — How do we want to remember Dina after today?

  — What would people like to happen after this meeting?

  — Is there anyone we need to talk with? Who shall do this? What needs to be said?

— How do we want to go on from here?

We created an opportunity for all the staff to participate in the re-membering of the child's life and relationships on the ward, inviting the ward team to co-memorate the life of the dead child rather than mourn their death. These sessions were generally very well attended, and some ward staff reported the value of this sort of collective remembering which connected them with, rather than distanced them from, their colleagues on the ward. Whereas staff support groups, set up with the intention of mourning the death, seemed to exclude those who were not previously involved with the child, co-memorating specifically invited—and hence involved—anyone who wanted to participate in celebrating the life, living, and relationships of the child. Co-memorating, therefore, does not require the participants involved to have had personal or direct experience of the re-membered events or relationships.

> Since Tania V had arrived unconscious on the ward, the staff could reflect only on her beauty and the serenity surrounding her, which evoked images of Sleeping Beauty. Mrs V had remarked that there was no one else in this country who "really" knew Tania except for herself and Miriam. Hence, after Tania died we invited Mrs V and Miriam to join us in co-memorating Tania's life through sharing stories of Tania from different times and places.

Although the staff were able to contribute only a limited perspective on Tania's life and relationships, co-memorating with Mrs V and Miriam enabled them to elaborate a fuller story of Tania's life and to participate in the *"party"* to celebrate her sister that Miriam had been wanting. In conversation with interested others, mother and daughter were able to re-member Tania from past times and places. Through co-memorating with the ward team they were therefore able to construct a narrative of their life with Tania which they could take on to in-form their futures.

Creating a context from which to act

The process of co-memorating therefore involves re-membering the past into the present so that a context can be created from which to act towards the future. This context of interwoven memories and narratives is essential to the identity and integrity of the family, community, and individual. In this way our memories and stories from different contexts become our "selves", in-forming versions of who we were, who we are, and who we might become.

Miriam and Mrs V were able to use the ward team to help them interweave their memories from past times and places with their present narratives and future possibilities. Beth, on the other hand, sought help at a time in her life when she experienced an absence of memories to in-form her self.

Beth had been 13 when her mother died. Beth sought therapy shortly before her 38th birthday, complaining that she had "not been myself" and was feeling "directionless". Early on in our meeting she told me that her mother had died at 38. When I asked about the connection between her mother's death at 38 and her deciding to seek therapy close to her 38th birthday, Beth told me that she had always "used her as a guide" and recently felt that she could not "remember her any more".

I began to wonder what had happened to those memories and narratives relating to her mother that had previously "guided" and in-formed Beth. It seemed as if Beth were now without a context from which to act. Working with the idea that memories evolve with use and gain new meanings when used in different relation-ships, I began to explore how Beth was currently "using" her memories of her mother and what opportunities she had for co-memorating.

An only daughter and middle child, Beth told me that she could speak quite openly about her mother with her father and two brothers. When I asked if there were other women in her family who might offer alternative "guidance", she referred only to an estranged great-aunt on her mother's side. I wondered what her mother had made of the prevalence of so many men in their family, whether she preferred relationships with men or whether she found opportunities with women outside the family. Beth referred to a few very good friends of her mother. Although she had not had contact with them since she was about 18, she knew where to find them and was interested in the ideas that they might have on how her mother would have liked to live her life, had she survived; what opportunities she might have created for herself; and what choices she might have made. I had offered the option to Beth of inviting these women to our sessions in the centre, but she preferred to take up this project on her own and met with me again after she had talked with her mother's friends.

Beth: They were thrilled to see me—so many tears. They were exactly how I remembered them—hadn't changed a bit.

Glenda: Did you talk about your mother together?

Beth: A lot.

Glenda: Like what?

Beth: They told me lots of things I'd forgotten. Well . . . I remembered when they said. They talked so much, not always agreeing. At first I was so confused—I started to think "what was real?" I wish I'd recorded the sessions—now I see why you do. How do remember everything here?

Glenda: How did you remember?

Beth: Then I let myself swim in it. We laughed a lot, too.

Glenda: And what did you come away with—have you taken something more of your mum so you can carry on?

Beth: I was terribly upset at first—I've always thought of her as so creative and different and wild in a way.

Glenda: And now?

Beth: Well, Laura seemed to think she'd always wanted grand-children—I'd never thought of mum as a grandmother.

Glenda: And if you did now—how would that affect what you might do?

Beth: You're probably thinking I'll go get pregnant or something.

Glenda: Is that what you'd like?

Beth: I don't know—it's not an option at the moment. Can't imagine mum so staid.

Glenda: You said you were upset at first—how has meeting with your mum's friends helped?

Beth: I've been having this idea that I need mum to tell me what I should do next—it's not as if she's been doing that for the last twenty-six years—crazy.

Glenda: And now?

Beth: (*laughs*) I liked hearing what she could be thinking—I know it's only "could be". It's not as if Laura can read her mind or has some direct line—though the way she talks you would think she has. Wish I could speak with such authority on everything and anything.

Glenda: So Laura and the other women . . .

Beth: Jean and Anna.

Glenda: . . . they've given you a few ideas about life beyond 40?

Beth: That's what I was thinking—my mum could have thought I should get married and have kids or whatever—I probably would have done what I wanted anyway—it was good to see them lot again, know what I mean . . . yeah, maybe they did give me a few ideas. I was worried I might change my mind about mum. I did in a way but she feels more real now.

Memories could be looked at as narratives within a context, so that when the context changes to a different relationship, time, or place, the narrative deconstructs, creating possibilities for different versions to be told and for new meanings to emerge. Sharing memories in a different context, which included her mother's friends instead of her family, Beth notes that she "changed her mind" about her mother with the deconstruction of her familiar narratives. She goes on to reflect how the different stories about her mother in turn change her relationship with her mother, who becomes "more real" for her.

It may have been that certain memories of her mother could not be re-membered within the narratives that Beth was able to create with the men in her family. Through co-memorating with a group of older women friends of her mother, however, she could re-collect old and familiar memories of her mother that she had not "used" for some time. By connecting these past stories to her present within the context of these different relationships, Beth could go on to give new and useful meanings to some of her old memories and thereby create a context from which to act. Thus memories and stories from her different contexts could become her "selves", not only in-forming versions of who she was, but also who she might become. Co-memorating therefore creates the opportunity to revisit old selves and evolve new selves through sharing and creating stories that incorporate the deceased.

Re-membering lost selves

Co-memorating with her mother's women friends enabled Beth to reconstruct her relationship with her mother and thereby reconnect with old and familiar versions of herself. Hence she could go on to in-form her self and create opportunities for new selves to emerge.

> Eight months after Tania died, Miriam told me, "Now I cannot be a sister". At that time, Mrs V was asking for advice because Miriam was spending "too much time" in her room talking to herself. She had told her mother on several occasions that Tania had "come to play" and they were "doing things" together. The school reported that Miriam was "withdrawn" and was becoming increasingly "isolated".

Miriam had lost her relationship with Tania, and I took her words, "Now I cannot be a sister", to mean that she was experiencing a loss of her "sister-self". I began to wonder whether her "doing things" together with Tania created an opportunity for Miriam to reconnect with her sister-self and thought of asking her and her mother questions that might bring forth those versions of her selves that had been missing to her through the death of Tania and the loss of their sister relationship.

> Glenda: Mrs V, what did Tania see when she looked at Miriam through loving eyes? [White, 1989b]
>
> Mrs V: Miriam was like a mother to Tania.
>
> Glenda: Did she look after her?
>
> Mrs V: (nods)
>
> Glenda: How? What did she do?

Mrs V: She took care of her . . . sometimes she was too much in charge . . . not punish . . .

Glenda: Bossy? Strict?

Mrs V: Yes strict. They played very well.

Glenda: So they were also friends? Good friends?

Mrs V: Very good friends. Very good friends.

(*Mrs V is crying, while Miriam looks out the window.*)

Glenda: Miriam, do you still see Tania these days?

Miriam: Mmm . . .

Glenda: Is that good?

Miriam: Mmm . . .

Glenda: How? What is it like? Can you tell me?

Miriam: Good.

Glenda: I see. And what does Tania think about you? If Tania was here now, what really good things would she tell us about you—that she really likes about you?

Miriam: I let her be the baby—and then I cuddle her.

Glenda: Do you like that? So do you like to be the baby—or the mummy or the daddy?

Miriam: (*laughs*)   The mummy.

Glenda: Mmm . . . And what about a friend—do you like to be a friend with Tania?

Miriam: (*nods*)

Glenda: Can you be the mummy these days—if you are not playing with Tania?

Miriam: No.

Glenda: Do you have any friends at school who will let you be the mummy?

In relationship with her sister Tania, Miriam was able to "be" both mother and friend. Since the death of her sister, Miriam had found no other living context within which her sister-self, which incorporated aspects of her "mother-self and her "friend-self", could emerge. Having established with Miriam that she valued those versions of her self and would like to find ways to keep them alive and enjoy them with other people outside her family, we could go on to explore alternative contexts, including school and social clubs that might create opportunities for those missed versions of her self to emerge.

Beth said she had not been herself recently and that she had lost her memories of her mother. Miriam remarked that she could not "be" a sister any more, following the death of her sibling. Mrs E told me that the family "have not been ourselves since nan died". These people were reflecting their disorientation in response to the loss of versions of their selves following the death of significant people in their lives with whom they had participated in formative relationships. Through re-membering and co-memorating with family, community, or helping professionals, they were able to reconnect with those relationships. Hence they were able to construct new versions of their lost selves within their re-membered relationships.

CHAPTER 6

Elaborating stories and extending abilities: training and supervision

I hold a preferred story that "death talk does not necessarily require professional expertise" and that "personal knowledges offer valuable contributions to people who are dying or be-reaved". Hence during learning events on death and bereavement, I do not choose to position myself as holding superior or exclusive knowledges on these subjects. To do this might imply that I am informing less knowledgeable participants on loss, grief and mourning and might risk subjugating their personal, cultural or religious knowledges at the outset. Instead, I prefer to share the responsibility for knowing about death, mourning, and grieving among those who participate out of an interest in learning, which includes myself. As trainer, I take responsibility for introducing new ideas from my personal and professional perspectives when possible, and for helping participants make connections between their own ideas, theories, and practice. I therefore expect to experi-ence the training session as mutually in-forming.

The exercises presented in this chapter are intended to enable all participants involved in training sessions to explore and elaborate their stories of death and bereavement, value their abilities, and extend their practices through sharing and mutually validating their knowledges and competences. The exercises can be performed by individuals on their own. However, opportunities for learning can be enhanced if participants use the exercises to generate conversations in relationships with others.

If a group of people chooses to work on an exercise together, I suggest that participants agree a contract of roles and responsibilities at the start. This may include an agreement about confidentiality and how the learning from the exercise might be used. I have also noticed that the working and the learning of the group can be helped by designating facilitators from within the group to take responsibility for setting up and leading the exercises, asking the questions, managing time, inviting connections between feedback and some of the theoretical ideas suggested at the end of each exercise, as well as ensuring that each participant has a fair chance to participate. The facilitator's role can be rotated at the end of each exercise, and sharing the role within a pair gives two facilitators the opportunity to participate in the exercises with each other. Facilitation of the exercises need not require or assume expertise.

Exploring beliefs
and elaborating stories

Many participants who have attended my workshops have told me that they have never had the opportunity to articulate openly their own ideas about death or mourning. Exercises 1 to 3 invite participants to explore stories and theories in conversation with each other and may be of interest to those who would like to join with others in extending their thinking about death and bereavement. These exercises are therefore not intended to teach participants about death, how to grieve or mourn, or how best to work with the bereaved or dying. Instead they are intended to create opportunities for participants to explore their own beliefs, to elaborate their repertoires of personal and professional narratives about death, dying, and bereavement, and to practise talking about death with others.

EXERCISE 1   EXPLORING AND ELABORATING STORIES

- Participants are invited to explore their beliefs about death in pairs with questions like:
— How do you explain death to yourself?
— Which ideas about death are you most comfortable with?
— What do you believe happens:
  . . . when people die?
  . . . after people die?

- Feedback is taken in the whole group, and as many different ideas as possible are recorded on flip-charts. The facilitator takes a non-evaluative stance throughout the sharing of these ideas in an attempt to create an atmosphere of increasing trust in which participants are encouraged to respect differing points of view.

- The facilitator may choose to elaborate further a repertoire of stories with the group by presenting or eliciting additional beliefs, stories, and theories from different sources. For example, participants may be asked to consider other views that they have met from family, culture, religion, clients, or training. I have also presented courses with a selection of (anonymous) views from previous course participants and quotations from religious, cultural, or philosophical literature and have made children's storybooks about death available.

I have found that this exercise helps to create an atmosphere of mutual respect at the start of a training event. Having shared their beliefs and stories in a non-judgemental context, participants often feel more comfortable to explore their own doubts, as well as ideas to which they are strongly committed, throughout the session.

Having validated personal stories of death, grieving, and mourning, I may go on to present psychological, developmental, or other professional theories about death, bereavement, and mourning, such as those described in Chapters Two and Three and in Appendix A, setting the context with a comment like "and here is another set of ideas to add to those we have already shared".

Chapter Two also reviews a range of beliefs about death and dying contributed by participants attending some of my courses, and Appendix B examines some of the beliefs about death and mourning reflected in a selection of books on death for children.

Feedback from this exercise can be used to illustrate the multiplicity of views and beliefs held by individuals or within groups of people. Hence the exercise could open space for discussion on the implications of the diversity of views about death and bereavement for communication among families and staff groups.

The questions described above relate to theories and explanations of death. The same exercise could be adapted to explore and elaborate participants' ideas and theses on a range of other themes relating to bereavement. For example, questions for participants to address stories about "talking about death" could be generated from my conversations about death talk with families in Chapter One, and questions to explore mourning stories could be developed from conversations and ideas about mourning tasks and practices presented in Chapter Three.

Participants could consider the use of the questions in this exercise for exploring with clients, children, and families their beliefs and stories about death. They could also be invited to generate additional questions to explore a range of issues related to death, grief, and mourning. Further approaches to generating and extending repertoires of stories are presented in Chapter Four.

EXERCISE 2   WHERE DO OUR STORIES COME FROM?

• Participants are invited to brainstorm where their different beliefs and stories about death and mourning come from, who might share those ideas, and who might hold different ones

• The contexts identified are listed on a board, and the facilitator may choose to add examples to include both personal and professional contexts—for example, life and death experience, family, culture, religion, training, profession, education, gender.

• Participants may be asked to reflect on which stories they draw from which contexts and which stories or ideas they prefer.

This exercise draws attention to the contexts that inform the stories and beliefs that we hold, and it may be used in conjunction with Exercise 1. The facilitator may point out that it is not uncommon for one person to hold a number of contradictory beliefs or for members in a family or staff group to hold several different views. The exercise also creates the opportunity to discuss which stories or knowledges are privileged and how that comes about. The facilitator might also want to raise the idea that this "multiverse" of beliefs and stories could present us with richness of choice as well as confusion.

EXERCISE 3   BECOMING AN OBSERVER TO OUR OWN BELIEFS

• Participants are invited to select four or five contexts and to write down the beliefs and stories about death or mourning that they draw from those contexts.

• Sharing their written exercises in twos or threes, they then discuss, with each other,

. . . are the stories the same or similar?

. . . are there any that are very different or seem to contradict each other?

. . . how well do the stories fit together?

. . . what happens and what do you do when the stories fit well or contradict each other?

When I participated in this exercise with a colleague, I wrote:

"*My culture*: Mourning rituals are helpful; it is better to grieve in groups.

My psychology training: I should help bereaved people grieve appropriately, e.g. using Guided Mourning techniques; pathological grief differs from non-pathological bereavement; stages of grief offer a useful way of conceptualizing the mourning process.

My training in systemic therapy: there is no right way to mourn; staying connected to the client's feedback is good practice.

My experience with families: people grieve in different ways; bereavement affects family relationships; grief is a unique experience.

My Personal Experience: talking is helpful; everyone grieves in their own ways and time.

My Department/Manager: death and bereavement are not a problem but a natural life event, therefore only pathological bereavement cases are appropriate referrals; since the child is dead we cannot register the case in an open file, and since we have to register all cases we cannot offer a bereavement service if the child is dead.

My Paediatric Ward Team: We need a bereavement service for all families who have lost a child on the ward, and the psychologist should develop this."

My colleague helped me to identify possible discrepancies and contradictions between the stories from my different contexts: for example, "we should diagnose and treat pathological bereavement" (psychology training and management contexts), "families show different ways of grieving" (experience with families and personal contexts), and "*all* families who have lost a child need a bereavement service" (paediatric ward team context).

This exercise offers participants a practical illustration of how an individual person, family, or staff team can hold a number of contradictory beliefs and discrepant stories at one time. The exercise also offers the opportunity for participants to look at the fit or coherence of their own personal and professional stories. A facilitator might point out that since our beliefs influence our actions, we may find ourselves torn between acting in different ways when influenced by contradictory beliefs, and he or she may invite participants to give examples of such situations to explore with the group.

A group of colleagues helped me to make sense of a certain confusion and discomfort I was experiencing in my work with families at the time of doing this exercise. For example, I had been bemused by the way I had approached the meeting with Mrs and Mr D, who had lost their long-awaited test-tube baby (Chapter

One). I could not understand why I had immediately launched into treating the couple as if they had the "problem" as defined by the referring paediatrician, when my usual practice was to start with the clients' perspectives on the referral and thereby clarify and create, together with the clients, a context for our meeting.

My colleagues suggested that my behaviour with Mr and Mrs D may have been guided by the stories from my department/manager, and from my psychology training contexts. In retrospect, I was helped to notice that my usually preferred stories from my systemic training and from my clinical and personal experience contexts were exerting only a weak influence on my actions, and that I was indeed privileging the stories about mourning and bereavement from my training and department contexts. I went on with my colleagues to explore how I felt pulled between my dual loyalties to these stories, which created confusion when I tried to act: in order to justify my service to my manager/department, I would need to identify "pathological bereavement", and in order to work ethically as a systemic therapist, I would need both to respect each person's unique way of grieving and avoid a normative pathologizing stance. Therefore if I approached bereavement as the "problem" I could not create a context of shared meaning with the couple, whereas if I did not identify pathological bereavement or an "acceptable" problem I could not justify my involvement with bereaved families to my manager, and if I did not offer a service to these families I would be undermining the efforts of my paediatric-ward team.

I recognized that to resolve what I experienced as a "no-win" situation for myself, I would need to find ways of foregrounding my clinical and personal stories in a way that avoided conflict in my relationship with my manager, or I would need to edit or rewrite some of my stories so that they could fit more comfortably with each other and with these different contexts. One colleague suggested that I attribute a new and different meaning to the families' attendance at sessions; for example, that "bereaved families come to see me because there is a conversation they need or want to have". Another colleague added that I could make the stories of my manager coherent with my team by suggesting that we "pilot" a "preventative service" and evaluate it through "research" by inviting families back to reflect on its use and their coping at follow-up.

EXERCISE 3A

• A facilitator could extend Exercise 3 by inviting participants to:

— Identify situations where professional theories, guidelines or policy conflicted with your personal beliefs:

. . . what did you do?

. . . which views did you privilege?

. . . what informed your action?

. . . what sense do you make of that now?

. . . if you did not have those professional views, what ideas might have informed you?

The facilitator could connect participants' feedback to a discussion about the effects of subjugating our personal and cultural stories to professional stories, illustrating with examples like Sister Lin in Chapter One, whose belief that "good practice requires giving precedence to professional views" dominated her relationship with her dying patient.

EXERCISE 3B

A staff team could adapt Exercise 3 to explore the fit between the beliefs of various staff members in relation to working with a particular child or family. Having identified and considered their different beliefs, team members could work in pairs to address the constraints and opportunities of their differences and ways to approach consistencies or contradictions between beliefs and stories.

Valuing our stories and abilities

Opportunities for learning can be created through supervision and self-reflexive experiences, as I show below.

Using our beliefs as a resource

Exercise 3 reflects how a person or team can hold several contradictory sets of beliefs about death and dying. Interaction with different people or situations can bring forth different aspects of such beliefs which have the potential to facilitate or hinder the process of a conversation or relationship. People have described their personal or professional beliefs as obstacles in their relationships with dying or bereaved patients or clients. In Chapter One, for example, Sister Lin perceived her personal "life experience" stories about death and mourning as impeding her relationship and work with her dying patient, Mrs W. In the same chapter, my communications with Dina B's mother and with Ms J show how a helper might use her own beliefs about death and mourning as a resource for conversations with others about death and dying. Below I invite a psychologist, in his supervision session, to explore how he might use his potentially contradictory beliefs as a resource for his work with a dying child, family, and hospital staff involved in his care.

> The psychologist reported that nursing and medical staff on the paediatric ward had asked him to speak to 11-year-old Nigel about his dying. The psychologist was concerned that he might be avoiding talking to the child and wanted me to tell him whether he was "chickening out". He described feeling very uncomfortable with the "tension on the ward", where he felt caught between several conflicting possibilities of what to do and what to believe.

We began by noting the **people and relationships involved in the issue of concern**—"talking with Nigel about his prognosis":

> The psychologist named the family (which included Nigel, his mother, and his father) and the hospital team—in particular, the nurses, the doctors, and himself.

We went on to address the psychologist's **own beliefs, theories, or theses related to the issue of concern:**

> He preferred not to talk about death if he "had the choice" but believed at the same time that "not talking is chickening out".

We addressed **where these beliefs came from:**

> He said that his preference to not talk came from his personal experience; he saw "talking about death as painful" and was not sure that he could "bear it" at that moment. His "not talking is chickening out" belief came from his professional training, which had taught him that it was "good practice to be available for the child" and that "children need an advocate".

I then asked him to review **the beliefs and messages of others involved,** including the family and his colleagues:

> *Glenda:* Who has asked you to talk to Nigel?
>
> *Psychologist:* The nurses and doctors on the ward.
>
> *Glenda:* Any idea what they are expecting you to say to him?
>
> *Psychologist:* Talk about dying, death . . .
>
> *Glenda:* Is he dying—have they told you that?
>
> *Psychologist:* The nurses say he is alert and wasting—his bowel has stopped functioning altogether . . .
>
> *Glenda:* And what are the doctors saying about his prognosis at the moment?
>
> *Psychologist:* His condition is not compatible with life.
>
> *Glenda:* Are they asking you to broach his dying with him?
>
> *Psychologist:* They have said that this is not terminal care. Am I chickening out? I want to know if I am avoiding talking to him. I know I have to watch that in myself. It's something I'd rather not do if I had a choice.
>
> *Glenda:* What is Nigel's mother's view?
>
> *Psychologist:* She doesn't want me to ask him questions about death because he'll give up. She says he will die sooner.

Glenda: And his father . . . what does he say?

Psychologist: He wants to hope—to focus on Nigel's health. He wants the ward staff to focus on Nigel's living—and the staff don't want to give false hope.

Glenda: Does Nigel want to talk to you—or someone?

Psychologist: He's not asking—but he is very ill, sleeping most of the time; angry and irritable when he's awake.

Together we addressed the **fit between the different messages and beliefs of all those involved** and concerned about talking with Nigel. Were they similar or complementary or did they contradict?

The psychologist noticed several contradictions between the messages he was receiving from the family and from the ward team. The doctors were saying that Nigel's bowel had "stopped functioning altogether", and his condition was "not compatible with life"; they also stated that "this is not terminal care, so we are not treating the child as if he is dying". The nurses had described Nigel as "alert and wasting". Nigel's father wanted to "focus on living and hope" and wanted Nigel to "be resuscitated" if his heart stopped. His mother believed that "talking with Nigel about his dying would invite death or lead to his giving up"; she did "not want him resuscitated" if his heart stopped. The ward team had asked the psychologist to "talk with the child". Although the contradictions between different messages of the family and the team (talk/don't talk; Nigel is dying/Nigel is not dying) could offer the psychologist alternatives for action, his belief that "not talking is chickening out" constrained him from seeing those alternatives as "choices".

When I asked him to anticipate or guess **which beliefs might dominate during work** with this child and family,

the psychologist was concerned that his "death-talk-is-painful" belief might take over, so that he would avoid talking about death with Nigel and the family.

We also explored **the possible effects on actions, thoughts, and**

feelings of the different beliefs and messages that he had identified, with questions like:

— How would you prefer to respond to the message from Nigel's mother/father/medical team?

— What do you think they are asking you to do?

— If you believed (that message), what would you most likely do?

— What do you see as the advantages/disadvantages of responding in this way for you/Nigel/his mother/father/the ward team?

The psychologist reported that he would be uncomfortable going against Nigel's parents' wishes and would feel "too pushy to insist on talking". He felt frustrated with the medical team for not being "clear". Although he preferred not to talk to Nigel if he had the "choice", he did not like seeing himself as "chickening out" and would feel he had failed the child.

Having identified some of his beliefs about talking about death, I invited the psychologist to explore how he might **use these theses as a resource to guide the work** with the child and family.

Glenda: You've described a number of ideas you have about talking with Nigel and his family. Could we **summarize the different ideas** you have mentioned? We could write them down. For example, sometimes you believe that "insisting on talking is too pushy". You also think that "avoiding talk is chickening out". And . . . ?

Psychologist: "Talking is painful", we discussed that. But I agree that "children need the chance to talk".

Glenda: Which of these ideas, or aspects of your **beliefs, would you like to keep? And what would you like to discard?**

Psychologist: I could get rid of the idea that "avoiding talk is chickening out".

Glenda: Is this discarded belief similar to, or does it go well with, any of the other beliefs you have mentioned here? **Does it contradict or conflict with any of your other ideas?**

Psychologist: Well it sort of contradicts "talking is too painful" and also "insisting on talking is pushy" . . . I suppose. But it goes well with "children need a chance to talk", since the child needs an advocate.

Glenda: Let's try and **look at the belief you discarded from different perspectives.** For example, what are the **advantages or disadvantages of this belief, its opposites, its alternatives.**

Psychologist: If I hang on to that idea that avoiding talking about death is chickening out, I become quite critical of myself and then I feel bad about what I'm doing, but I suppose there is an advantage in that I am more self-aware.

Glenda: Of what in yourself?

Psychologist: How I feel. If I let go of thinking that not talking about it with Nigel is chickening out, I could feel better if I don't talk, but then maybe I don't give him the chance to talk.

The psychologist saw his "avoiding-talking-about-death-is-chickening-out" belief as interfering with his feeling good about his work with this family and encouraging him towards being *"too pushy"*. However, he also thought that this belief could be useful in sharpening his *self-awareness* and giving the child a *chance to talk.*

Going on to consider **the influence of this exploration on thinking and possible actions,** the psychologist reported that he had begun by experiencing his belief that "avoiding death talk is chickening out" as a source of tension in his work with Nigel and his parents. By taking different perspectives on that belief, considering its advantages and disadvantages as well as its opposites, he was able to generate a set of alternative ideas about death talk, which included ideas about "pushing", enhancing "self-awareness", and creating a "chance to talk". He could then go on to **use these new themes to inform the work** he was doing with the child and family.

For example, the theme of "pushing" informed the psychologist's decision to ask the family questions about their views on talking about death, speaking with Nigel, and what sort of talking they might consider comfortable or "too pushy". His theme of "self-awareness" encouraged him to address personal and professional beliefs about death talk with the ward staff. He also began to wonder about Nigel's awareness of his health status, what he knew, and what he might want to know, and he went on to ask the parents whether he could ask Nigel if he had any questions or was worried about anything. The "chance-to-talk" theme drew his attention to the notions of "opportunity" and "choice", so that he later asked the parents some hypothetical questions, such as: "If he thought he was dying, what might Nigel want now? If you knew he was well, what would you want to be doing now? If you knew he was going to die, what would you be wanting to do or have done?"

I have highlighted here guidelines for approaching our own beliefs as resources for conversations with others about death and dying in situations that might feel stuck, unclear, or troubled by the sort of "tension" described by the psychologist working with Nigel. Although one's repertoire of ideas is usually enriched by using the guidelines in conversations with others, people working alone can ask those questions of themselves. I have addressed these questions in personal dialogue with myself and have noticed that I am most likely to lose interest, run out of ideas, or get stuck when I touch upon beliefs or theses to which I am particularly attached. Asking myself **"What level of context am I relating to at the moment?"** and **"What context level could I move to?"** has sometimes inspired me to take a fresh perspective. In Chapter One, for example, I was working with Ms J in the context of her family. Reviewing our communication, I moved to the contexts of race and culture, which gave me another perspective on our work together and generated new ideas to inform future conversations.

Initially the psychologist and I were relating to the contexts of his paediatric staff team and Nigel's family and recognized that we had been foregrounding his professional contexts. I remarked that the psychologist had associated his "talking-is-painful" belief with his personal experience. He was interested in exploring whether the context of his personal experience could give us new ideas for working with Nigel, his family, and the staff team.

Glenda: You have learnt from your personal experience that talking is painful?

Psychologist: Yes.

Glenda: What else has your personal experience shown you? For example, how did you manage talking and pain? Or what did you learn about talking and pain?

Psychologist: Time . . . it was all about timing.

Glenda: Do you mean the right time to talk about dying?

Psychologist: You lose sense of time. It all blurs, so you think you have to sort it all out immediately. When you realize you can't—I mean, there are some things you cannot even know—then you try to simplify it all.

Glenda: How?

Psychologist: I don't know . . . like saying to yourself, this is not happening.

Glenda: Or?

Psychologist: This will sound awful . . . but wishing it would end right now so at least you know what's happening, or you can get on with it without the awful waiting.

Both the psychologist and I were very moved by this conversation, which brought forth so many new themes that we had not previously considered in relation to Nigel and his carer network. The psychologist spoke with the family and with the ward team about their views on the "timing" of talking. He also asked how people were experiencing time. Whereas Nigel's parents felt "frozen" and had stopped thinking of the future at all, Nigel seemed to be talking a lot about the past, and the ward team were wanting to "fast forward and sort it all out". The psychologist later told me that introducing a time frame into his conversations with the family and the ward team seemed to "slow the ward down and unfreeze the family, so they moved into the same time zone in a way".

Our personal and professional identities

The psychologist working with Nigel described a complexity of intercommunication between the child, the family, and the medical and nursing team, so that reports of the child's health status were often contradictory or unclear. In Chapter Two, I address how the impending death of a child challenges the identity and relationships of children and their carers, including parents and professionals. When people are in conflict or confusion about acknowledging the child's impending death, versions of questions to explore the effects on identity presented in Chapter Two might offer carers the chance to create some clarity and hence open up possible ways to go on. For example, those caring for the child might consider:

— What is my main job/role in relation to this child or family?

— How does the child's health status affect my ability to do that job/my view of my role/how I see myself/my relationship with the child?

— What effect would my seeing the child as having a better/worse prognosis have on my job/my relationship with the child and family/how I see myself?

— Who can I become in relation to this child/family if I no longer perform that role?

The psychologist working with Nigel discussed some of these questions with his ward team. The nurses anticipated that their role with Nigel was unlikely to change much if they perceived him as dying, since they would still be involved in ensuring his comfort and quality of life on the ward. The doctors, however, anticipated quite different roles for themselves were they openly to acknowledge the child's dying with the family. One doctor told the psychologist: "We become redundant, don't we. He has to be transferred to the palliative care team." Soon after this conversation, the ward team requested a consultation from the palliative care team.

Extending practices

The following exercises offer participants the chance to practise the interviewing and questioning approaches presented in Chapters Two, Three, and Four.

Exercises 4 and 5 introduce participants to a method of questioning described in Chapter Three which involves joining the language of the interviewees and acknowledging and using the child's and the family's expertise.

EXERCISE 4   CONSTRUCTING EMOTIONS AND EXPLORING FEELINGS

Participants are asked to work in small groups of three or four.

• One "interviewee" in each small group is asked to relate a personal story where something happened and to describe their response (*I did ... and ...*) without naming how they felt.

• The other participants in the small groups then designate emotional descriptions to the interviewee's responses, talking about the interviewee in the third person: for example, "she was probably 'excited'"; "he seemed so 'distressed'").

• The participants, excluding the interviewee, agree on one of these feelings (the designated feeling) to explore in the interview.

• One person interviews the interviewee about the designated feeling, using the following questions:

— If you choose to describe your response as [the designated feeling], how does that affect how you see yourself/what you might do next?

— If you are helped to see yourself as [the designated feeling], what opportunities does this provide?

— Are there ways that describing yourself as [the designated self-description] gets in the way of things or creates difficulties for you/others?

— If you chose another feeling instead of [the designated feeling], what might you choose?

— What effect would [this new chosen self-description] have on you, your relationships, what you do?

• Feedback is taken from the interviewees, who are invited to discuss with each other in front of the group what it was like to be designated a feeling and their experience of the interview. The other participants are invited to comment on the process of selecting and designating an emotional description and on the process of the interview.

Feedback from Exercise 4 can be related to the ideas in Chapter Three, which propose that we construct emotional theories about

people's behaviour and bodily responses in order to make sense
of our feelings and inform ourselves or others about how to go
on. Exercise 4 gives participants the opportunity to experience the
effects of different emotional constructions. Participants could discuss the constraints and opportunities of being designated a feeling
in relation to the case examples reported in Chapter Three, where
children refuse the emotions constructed on their behalf by adults.

EXERCISE 5   CO-CONSTRUCTING EMOTIONS

In this exercise, participants can practise coordinating
communication about feelings without involving precise
descriptions of the emotions.

• Participants are asked to interview each other in pairs, with
one or two observers. The Interviewer says:

— Think of an event in which you have been involved, and
find the feeling that goes with what happened.

— Show me that feeling.

(Interviewees might choose to make it/do it/draw it/dance it.
The interviewer could ask for further descriptions of the feeling:
for example, "Where is it? How big is it? What colour is it? Is it
hot or cold, hard or soft?")

— How should we call it?

— What effect does [named emotion] have on your/others'
relationships?

— Has [named emotion] helped you? Got in the way? Could it
be useful to you or others?

— What do you want to do with it? (The interviewer could give
some examples, like: keep it/extend it/reduce it/change it
to ...)

— What do you think [others involved] think you should do
with [named emotion]?

— What is the next step you would like to take, and what needs
to happen to [named emotion] for you to be able to do that?

• Participants are asked to share their learning from the
interview.

The facilitator could invite reflection on the uses and effects of the questions and method of the interview. Participants could consider whether it was necessary for all persons in the interview to have exactly the same understanding of the feeling they were exploring. Feedback could be connected to ideas about the social construction of emotion presented in Chapter Three—in particular, the notion that to know the meaning of a word is to know how to use it and how to respond to it in a particular context.

EXERCISE 6   USING CHILDREN'S BOOKS

For this exercise, participants work in small groups of about four people.

• Each group selects a Story Reader and an Interviewer and is given one or two children's story books about death. (A selection of books on death for children is presented in Appendix B; I have attempted to include stories that reflect a diversity of beliefs and messages about death.)

• The Story Readers read the story to the rest of their group, who are asked to listen, with a view to sharing with each other those parts of the story about death that were especially meaningful to them.

• The Interviewer asks each member of the group:

— What is this story saying to you about death? (What happens when people die/after people die?)

— Which parts of the story do you prefer?

— Which parts do you want to keep or get rid of?

— What would you like to add?

• The Interviewer asks the group members to discuss the fit between their preferred stories, with questions such as:

— What are the similarities/differences between the ideas you each like?

— If we put together all the parts you each like the best, what do we get?

• The group spends some time creating a group story that fits for each member.

- Feedback can be taken on the content and process of this exercise:
    - small groups can relate the gist of the stories they have read, as well as comment on their possible meanings and uses for children and their carers;
    - participants can be invited to reflect on the process of co-creating a group story and how they might use this approach with children and families.

This exercise has many uses. It familiarizes participants with some of the children's literature on death and illustrates the diversity of theses about death implicit in different children's stories. It also invites participants to elaborate their repertoire of stories about death through a consideration of the ideas and theses reflected in the stories.

Participants are given the opportunity to practise coordinating and co-creating stories with a group. The facilitator can open discussion about the uses of this approach with children, families, and staff groups using the theory and practices presented in Chapter Four.

Exercise 6 can be extended so that participants can explore the fit of their small-group's chosen story with their own stories from their personal and professional contexts—for example culture, religion, and training. They may also address the implications of holding on to that newly co-created story for their relationships with others.

Acknowledging and knowing

When I join with participants in training, I begin by exploring their relationships with "knowledge" and with "knowing" so that I have some idea where to position myself in relation to their learning. I am therefore interested in what understandings they would like to get from the course, what sorts of learning they value, and which knowledges and abilities of their own they esteem and acknowledge. Are they expecting to leave the training session with more knowledges, fewer knowledges, or different knowledges? Are they expecting the trainer to have more, better, or different knowledges from their own?

At the start of a two-day training workshop on "The Care of the Dying Child", I asked a multidisciplinary group of fifteen participants working with sick children in hospital settings to tell me what they wanted from our working together, how they would know that they had got what they wanted, and who else would notice if they did get what they hoped for from the course. The participants, who included doctors, nurses, psychologists, teachers, and clergy, identified similar expectations. They wanted to learn about children's understanding of death, they wanted theories of mourning, they wanted "skills" and "tips" for what to do when working with dying or bereaved children and families in a range of different situations, they wanted demonstrations of what to say to dying patients, and they wanted to feel more confident working with the dying and bereaved by the end of the training session.

The participants preferred to talk of "bodies of knowledge" and went on to identify religious knowledge, cultural knowledge, and personal or experiential knowledge. The bodies of professional knowledge included medicine, education, psychology, psychoanalysis, behaviourism, and the "self-help sort". Few participants had anticipated "covering" personal knowledges on "a course like this". One doctor said that he had always thought of them as "getting in the way" since "to be professional one should be objective", which meant "keeping personal opinions out of work". Another participant expressed concern about imposing her religious views on patients. None of the participants had thought of using their personal beliefs as a resource. There was general agreement that they had come to this training event to learn psychological knowledge since I was a psychologist. There was a consensus that professional knowledges were more appropriate for use with clients in professional settings, which included hospitals and schools.

In the course of training, I also explore participants' relationship to learning and knowing. I am interested in whether they are expecting to be given definitive theories, content, information, and clear directives and whether they are interested in sharing their ideas and practices with each other. Are they expecting to explore and practise in a non-evaluative environment, and do they want to be assessed and told what to do and what not to do? What are their views of a convener of a workshop who may know less than they do about certain aspects of death and bereavement?

The course members above were keen to acquire "*theories*", "*models*", and "*skills*" and asked for handouts, reading lists, and "*guidelines*" to this end. Thus, like many participants on the short courses that I have convened, they showed most enthusiasm for the intellectual and practical, "what-to-think", "what-to-do", and "what-to-say" sorts of knowing, at the outset of the course. These participants also wanted to feel more "*confident*" by the end of the course. I was unsure how to make sense of this sort of knowing. Initially I had thought it might reflect their wish to extend their relational or bodily sorts of knowing to include "how to be with" dying or bereaved people or "how to use feelings" with the dying or bereaved (Andersen, 1995). However, they reported that few, if any, people would notice if they felt more confident and seemed to anticipate that a change in their confidence would entail a private or internal sort of knowing, involving relationship with self rather than relationship with others.

I used to respond to participants' emphasis on rational and practical knowing with a reluctance to teach psychological theories about death or present practical methods and techniques. I was guided by a belief that the presentation of information would be promoted to "truth" status, and I was concerned to avoid subjugating participants' personal knowledges (White & Epston, 1990) or perpetuating a view that there is a right way to mourn, grieve, die, or talk about death. Hence I avoided offering information to participants and instead invited them to generate their own material through training exercises that involved their participation in process and practice. However, my reticence to teach theories or provide practical instruction seemed to constrain my relationships with participants. I began to feel inhibited and unhappy by what I experienced as my self-censorship, and I wondered if I was frustrating their learning. I also sensed that some participants viewed me as withholding information. This discomfort shifted me to my present position in training, where I offer to share all the theories I have access to, not as truths within an implicit hierarchy of knowledges, but as possible stories that take their place among other theses—cultural, religious, communal, and professional. Instead of identifying any particular theory or story as the best or right way to work or think, therefore, I invite participants to evaluate different stories according to their own personal and professional contexts and those of the clients with whom they are working. Therefore throughout a course or workshop, I may pause with participants to consider the possible uses of a particular set of knowledges and the opportunities or constraints that it might present when working with different clients or in different contexts.

The subject of death itself evokes uncertainty: although we can be sure we will one day die, we do not know with absolute confidence when or how or why. Some participants may therefore be hoping that death/bereavement training might offer some degree of assurance or truth as a counterbalance to this uncertainty. Many of the exercises in this chapter, however, invite participants to generate a repertoire of alternatives rather than identify the right or wrong way to believe or proceed. Thus participants are expected to suspend knowing while they contemplate new and diverse possibilities. They are also asked to manage the uncertainty that frequently accompanies new learning. Some course participants have found it uncomfortable to spend too much time outside a "knowing space". If their professional background has supported a belief in certainties, the effect of questioning "truths" and acknowledging and experiencing contradictions can be particularly disorienting. Participants in these sorts of situations may insist that trainers present their views as a definitive model of what ought or should be adhered to, or they may insist on objectivity or truth.

> After generating a repertoire of beliefs about mourning with a course group using Exercise 1, a participant complained that she disliked "these random points" and insisted that I provide her with the "phylum and genus". When I looked up these words in the dictionary, both of their meanings related to classification and categorization and therefore connoted order and organization of information.

In these sorts of situation I might suggest that we all behave "as if we did not know or did not have a firm view on the matter" and explore what we might find out from this position before we go on to construct our categories and classifications. I might also reflect with participants about their views on the risks and benefits of knowing and uncertainty and enquire whether their professional position, experience, status, gender, or training influences their propensity to adopt a position of certainty and confidence or more of a deliberating and uncertain stance.

> Two participants described their status and professional position as "mere nurses" within their team and believed that their deliberating would be viewed as incompetence in a department that presented itself as a "centre of excellence". For those nurses, "excellence" implied being sure and "expert", and being "expert" required "being seen to know".

> * * *

> In Chapter Three, a trainee psychologist asked me what effect joining a child's language and acknowledging the child's and family's expertise would have on "our credibility with the medical profession". She believed that doctors and parents expected her to be an "expert" and that her failure to engage in medical discourse or present clear recommendations might suggest that she did not have "professional" abilities.

The two nurses above reflected that certainty affirmed their competence in relationships with colleagues, and the trainee psychologist had learnt that the languages of efficiency and technology communicate expertise within the hospital. Committed to upholding the reputation of excellence afforded their department, the nurses preferred to be certain rather than to deliberate. Committed to upholding the reputation of excellence afforded her profession, the psychologist hesitated to speak the language of the child, which she believed might challenge her credibility with her team. The exercises and supervision approaches presented in this chapter do not suggest that participants substitute their knowing for uncertainty, or that they supersede one language with another. Instead, the approaches are intended to offer participants opportunities to explore death, bereavement, and mourning from different perspectives and to develop their proficiencies with a multiplicity of languages for talking about death and dying.

Conclusion

When Mrs T (Chapter Four) asked me what she could tell her twin boys about the death of their father, I had expected to help the family create a coherent and meaningful story. Therefore when the family left their penultimate session with what seemed to me like a set of disconnected theses, I did not see our work together as "done". However, the T family showed me that the coherence of a narrative is not created in the therapy room. Instead it evolves in the course of its telling and its living. I could never have imagined the creative ways in which Daniel, Benjamin, and their mother went on to make use of the stories that we had explored in our sessions together.

Before I started writing this book, I had the idea that I could develop a general map that would direct me in my work with bereaved and dying children and families. Looking for connections and links between my experiences with clients and what seemed like disconnected theories about death and bereavement, I was working towards identifying patterns that might give meaning to specific instances. At that time, therefore, I was seeing each contact with a bereaved or dying child or family as another opportunity to create and refine my "working-with-death-and-dying" map. Although I was enjoying the sense of security and direction my emergent map was giving me, over time I began to recognize that I tended to follow the map at the expense of my relationship with my clients. I noticed how I was missing information they were giving me and losing connection with them, as my close attention to this map distracted me from attending to their feelings or following their communications that did not fit with or confirm it.

It was at this point that I decided to elaborate my existing repertoire of beliefs about death. Interest in learning different ideas about dying and bereavement re-awakened my curiosity, and I ventured away from the security of my familiar map towards new territory, as together with clients I explored possible death stories that might enable us to go on. Hence I closely connected with clients as we created new stories together, and I noticed how each new encounter with the dying or bereaved challenged my previously constructed map.

There have been times in the course of this sort of exploration that I have found myself bogged down amidst a confusing array of what seemed like too many unfamiliar and contradictory ideas, and, like the participant in Chapter Six, I have hungered for phylum and genus. In these sorts of situations, I have found it helpful to look for meaningful links between the collection of differing ideas and to abstract connecting themes to inform how I might go on. Moving back and forth between creating meaningful links and themes, evaluating their use with people in conversation, and allowing new ideas to challenge my previous themes towards creating new connections keeps me constantly in search of a balance between the complacency of the known, the discomfort of the unknown, and the wonder of the possible.

When I set about writing the conclusion to this book, I considered how I might use it to create a coherent narrative for the reader in which I might tie up loose ends. Then I recognized my pull towards phylum and genus. Hence I have decided to let my writing rest and remain wondering what the reader will make of these stories, theses, and loose ends. Having challenged one of my former premises—that our past determines our present and our present lays down the foundations for our future—I am now exploring such questions as, "What are the consequences for a lived life of having a different relationship with death?" and "How would our lives be different if, for example, we believe that there are many stories about what happens when people die and if we incorporate rather than exclude the diversity of views offered within a multicultural society?"

APPENDIX A

Some theories
of death and mourning

Developmental theories

Developmental theories of children's understanding of death commonly include the idea that a person's concept of death can be more or less complete and that a mature concept of death necessarily involves several different components, including the perception of death as a natural process which is final, irreversible, and universal. The conceptual underpinning of these theories has most frequently been Piagetian (1958), and researchers have sought to delineate ages and stages at which children acquire key components, with a view to establishing the age at which to expect full development of the concept. Kane (1979), for example, identified nine components of the death concept with ages at which they emerge. She reported that children between the ages of 3 and 5 years have a basic *realization* of the *separation* involved in death as well as the *immobility* of the dead person, although immobility may be seen as only partial and temporary. By 6 years, the child comprehends the *irrevocability of* death, has a notion that death induces *dysfunctionality,* and is beginning to make sense of the *causality* of death; by 7 years, the child recognizes the *universality* of death. Although, by 8 years children acknowledge the *insensitivity* of the dead person, according to Kane it is only by the age of 12 that they fully comprehend the effects of death on *appearance.*

There are large discrepancies in reports of the ages at which components of the death concept are acquired. The belief that death can be caused by magical thinking or by the behaviour or wishes of others, for example, is commonly described as typical of children around the age of 5, but is also noted in older children and adults who avoid talking about certain death-related issues lest they invite misfortune.

Recognition that acquisition of the meaning of death is not simply linear has encouraged several attempts to identify factors other than cognitive processes related to the development of a mature concept of death. Orbach, Gross, Glaubman, and Berman (1985), for example, show that understanding the meaning of death starts with the child's own experiences of death and reflects emotional and cultural factors.

Stage theory

In order to broaden understanding and awareness of the emotions experienced by dying people, Elizabeth Kubler-Ross (1970) described five stages of dying: *denial and isolation; anger; bargaining; depression; and acceptance*. The final stage of death is commonly interpreted as the last separation where the dying person needs to be able to let go of life with acceptance, and adults who cling to life are deemed unable to face death.

Phase theories

Colin Parkes (1972) describes grief as a process rather than a state or set of symptoms that start after a loss and then fade away. He portrays mourning as a succession of "clinical pictures" which blend into and replace one another in phases. Therefore *numbness*, the first phase, gives place to a second phase of pining and *yearning*, during which anger and irritability commonly feature. During the third phase, the mourner experiences disorganization and *despair*, and, for Parkes, it is only after this stage of depression that recovery and *reorganized behaviour* occurs.

Bowlby (1989) identifies *protest, despair,* and *detachment* as a sequence of responses characteristic of all forms of mourning. He also posits that the mourner needs to pass through the phases of *numbing, yearning and searching for the lost figure,* and *disorganization and despair* before mourning is finally resolved and *reorganization* is possible.

Task theory

Worden (1991) connects "tasks" of mourning with Freud's concept of grief *work* and identifies four tasks that must be accomplished for the process of mourning to be complete. He argues that identifying tasks is "more useful for the clinician" than stages or phases of mourning, since a "task" incorporates an end point and implies that something can be done, which is a powerful antidote to the helplessness affecting mourners. Worden identifies four goals of grief counselling to help the bereaved complete four tasks of mourning. I: to increase the *reality of the loss*; II: to help *deal with expressed and latent affect*; III: to help *overcome impediments to readjustment after the loss*; IV: to encourage *saying an appropriate goodbye and feeling comfortable reinvesting back in life.*

APPENDIX B

Books for children and young people

Below I present a brief synopsis of some books written for children on the subjects of death and dying. I review the death theses reflected in each story in terms of dimensions of the "mature concept" of death (e.g. finality, universality, dysfunctionality), as well as the dimensions that go "beyond the mature concept" of death (e.g. continuity, and connection) presented in Chapter Two. I also address each story's approach to mourning, grieving, and managing the effects of loss. The words in bold reflect the particular death theses and approaches to mourning emphasized in each story.

* Althea. (1982). *When Uncle Bob Died*. London: Dinosaur Publications.

  Death theses
  When Uncle Bob dies, the young boy in the story learns that death is caused by illness and old age, that it is **final** and **universal,** and that all function ceases.

  Having had the opportunity to remember his uncle by talking with his parents, he also learns how the dead person can **live on in our memories.**

Mourning

The mourners in the story experience both sadness and anger, and it is acknowledged that we sometimes pretend that the dead person will come back, to help ourselves feel better.

The family attends the funeral, where they are able to say goodbye. **Talking** and **remembering** Uncle Bob helps so that they can **carry on with life,** which includes times of joy and pleasure.

* Alumenda, S. (1994). *Thandiwe's Spirit and the River.* Harare: Baobab Books. [culture: African]

Death theses

Akedu's best friend, Thandiwe, has drowned in a river, which he visits daily in the hope of finding her **spirit which lives on.**

He takes comfort in the idea that he can connect with and **protect the spirit** of his little friend.

Mourning

This story gently reflects the grief in a small child who misses his friend.

* Ancona, G. (1993). *Pablo Remembers: The Fiesta of the Day of the Dead.* New York: Lothrop, Lee & Shepard Books. [culture: Mexican]

Death theses:

Pablo and his friends welcome visits from **the spirits of dead** children and adults with gifts, food, and lights during the festival of the Day of the Dead.

Mourning

Pablo is reassured that he will be able to connect with his dead grandmother by **celebrating her memory** and with those of all the ancestors through this annual **community ritual.**

* Burningham, J. (1984). *Granpa.* London: Picture Puffins.

Death theses

This story, about the close relationship between a small girl and her grandfather, who dies, ends with an illustration of granpa's empty chair, representing the **finality** of death.

The book does not overtly address what happens after a person dies, although the little girl's musing about heaven early on in the story creates an opportunity for an adult to go beyond the mature concept of death to talk with a child about continuity or connection after death.

Mourning
The effects of the loss and the process of grieving are not overtly addressed in this story.

- Crossland, C. (1989). *Someone Special Has Died.* London: St Christopher's Hospice.

  Death theses
  Death is described as **final and irreversible,** and dead people are described as insensitive to pain. The authors challenge magical thinking, emphasizing that nothing that the reader said, did, or felt would have made the deceased ill or die.

  Mourning
  The book **normalizes feelings** of sadness, crying, and guilt and explains how we might want to pretend that the death has not happened.

  Talking and remembering the deceased is considered helpful, and the funeral is presented as an opportunity to say goodbye.

- Jordan, M. (1989). *Losing Uncle Tim.* Morton Grove, IL: Albert Whitman and Company.

  Death theses
  Daniel understands that death is irreversible and that the dead person ceases to function when his loved Uncle Tim dies. His parents explain that his uncle's death is **caused** by AIDS and challenge his magical thinking that thoughts or behaviour might cause or prevent death.

  Daniel reflects on his mother's view that **part of the dead person lives on** in some way, and he is able to continue a relationship with his dead uncle through his involvement with the possessions, abilities, and stories inherited from him.

  Mourning
  Daniel shows fear, sadness, and **distress** in the course of Uncle Tim's dying and sometimes uses pretending to help himself to cope.

By **using his inheritance to remember** his dead uncle, he begins to have ideas for his future that reflect his identification with his uncle.

- Kusugak, M.A. (1993). *Northern Lights. The Soccer Trails.* Willowdale, Ontario: Annick Press.   [culture: Inuit]

Death theses
Kataujaq learnt that her mother's death, when she was very young, was caused by illness and that death was **irreversible** since she would never come home.

Her grandmother explained that her mother's soul left her body when she died and joined all the other **souls in heaven.**

Mourning
Kataujaq would cry with great **sadness** and loneliness when she thought of the death of her mother.

However, watching the Northern Lights, with the belief that she was witnessing and **connecting with the souls** of the dead playing soccer, gave her great comfort.

- Lanton, S. (1991). *Daddy's Chair.* Rockville, MD: Kar-Ben Copies. [culture: Jewish]

Death theses
When Michael's father dies, his mother helps him to learn that death is **final and irreversible,** and together they discuss the cause of his father's death.

Mourning
The **ritual** of observing the Jewish week of mourning creates an opportunity for Michael and his family to **remember and celebrate** Michael's father's life and to share their sadness at their loss. Michael finds ways of connecting with his father through sitting in his father's chair and sharing relationships, stories, and memories with people who were connected with him.

- Mellonie, B. & Ingpen, R. (1983). *Beginnings and Endings with Lifetimes In Between.* Limpsfield, Surrey: Dragon's World Ltd.

Death theses
This book illustrates that insects, fish, mammals, and people all have a lifetime, so that death is **part of the natural cycle** of all living

things. Caused by illness or injury at any age, death is therefore inevitable and universal.

Mourning
Loss, grief, and mourning are not addressed in this book.

- Nodar, C. S. (1992). **Abuelita's Paradise.** Morton Grove, IL: Albert Whitman & Company. [culture: Spanish/American]

  Death theses
  Marita's mother explains that her dead grandmother is in a sort of **paradise.**

  Mourning
  Sitting in her dead grandmother's rocking chair, Marita is able to **remember stories** that her grandmother told her before she died, which helps her to feel closer to her grandmother and her mother.

- Perkins, G., & Morris, L. (1992). *Remembering Mum.* London: A&C Black.

  Death theses
  When they feel sad about their mother's death, Sam's and Eddy's father tells them that they will always have her in their hearts.

  Mourning
  The little boys and their father express **sadness** and anger in relation to their mother's death. They are also able to **get on** with the routine of their lives and are able to find moments of joy and pleasure.

  Remembering their mother in different ways during the day helps the boys connect with her. Comfort, **cuddles, and closeness** with friends and family help them feel a lot better, so that life can go on.

- Rayner, C. (1978). *The Body Book.* London: Piccolo Picture Books.

  Death theses
  In the last chapter of this book, "Growing Old and Dying", death is portrayed as universal, inevitable, and **part of the natural cycle** of living things, and the cause of death is attributed to illness and the inevitable effects of tiredness and wear in old age.

  It is explained that **dead people become part of new people** in different ways: through their return to the earth and contribution to the food cycle and via the feelings and memories of the dead that are passed on to children through learning.

Mourning
Sadness and crying are presented as normal responses in mourning for children and adults, and funerals are presented as an opportunity to say goodbye to the deceased.

- Stickney, D. (1982). *Water Bugs and Dragonflies—Explaining Death to Children.* London: Mowbray.

Death theses
Once water bugs become dragonflies, they are unable to rejoin their water bug friends below the surface of the water again, in much the same way as death is **irreversible** for humans.

This story uses the analogy of the water bug's short life underwater as humans' time on earth, and their emergence as dragonflies into the bright sunlit world above the water, where there are many other dragonflies, as humans' **life after death,** with the opportunity to reconnect with the deceased in a place something like heaven.

Mourning
The effects of loss and the process of grieving are not overtly addressed in this story.

- Varley, S. (1984). *Badger's Parting Gifts.* London: Collins Picture Lions.

Death theses
Old age was the cause of Badger's death, which was likened to his falling out of his body and leaving it behind as he embarked on a **journey** down a long tunnel.

Each of his animal friends could hold on to a special memory of him through recounting the abilities he had passed on to them. In this way Badger **lives on in the memories** of others.

Mourning
Although his friends were very sad and tearful at his death, talking about Badger and **sharing what they had learnt** from him helped them feel better.

Children and families cross-referenced

Georgie H

Georgie was diagnosed with a malignant brain tumour when he was 3 years old. Following surgery, chemotherapy, and radiotherapy, he enjoyed two years of good health before a sudden regrowth of the tumour. Progress and spread of the cancer halted Georgie's education only three months after he started attending school. He died shortly after his sixth birthday, and his mother sought help for her concerns about the effects of Georgie's death on his 3-year-old sister, Lisa.

Daniel and Benjamin T

Mrs T and her 9-year-old twin boys, Daniel and Benjamin, met with me following the death of the boys' father. Mr T had died unexpectedly five months previously while the boys were away at boarding school. The family's doctor had requested help for Daniel, who "was talking incessantly to his father throughout the night". Mrs T had started attending spiritualist meetings after her husband's death.

Monica L
CHAPTER 1: 8–9   CHAPTER 2: 31–32, 37   CHAPTER 4: 64

Nine-year-old Monica L had been diagnosed with leukaemia when she was 4. Intensive chemotherapy enabled her to participate fully in school, family, and social life for a good three years before her energy and health deteriorated quite rapidly when she was 9. Monica's father was referred to me, by the haematologist treating Monica, because of concerns that Mr L was setting Monica school work and "refusing to acknowledge" that she was dying.

Dina B
CHAPTER 1: 9–10, 14, 18–19   CHAPTER 2: 21–22, 24–25, 29–30, 36–37
CHAPTER 5: 90–91   CHAPTER 6: 107

Four-year-old Dina B had been sent home for terminal care. She had been treated for bowel cancer with surgery, chemotherapy, and radiotherapy since she was 2. She lived with her parents and two imaginary friends, Skimpy and Squonk. Mr and Mrs B were originally from Thailand and were practising Buddhists.

The J family
CHAPTER 1: 14–17   CHAPTER 2: 29   CHAPTER 6: 107, 112

Ms J lost her 3-month-old baby, Tyrone, a cot death. She attended her first appointment with her remaining children, Tyrone's twin sister, Tonisha, Nicole (8 years) and Marisa (2 years). Ms J was feeling supported by her friend, Bernice, who had also lost a child. She described herself and her children as Black British.

Miriam and Tania V
CHAPTER 3: 44–45, 46–47, 48   CHAPTER 5: 78–83, 84, 92–93, 96–98

Seven-year-old Tania V died on the paediatric ward within a week of admission with an inoperable malignant brain tumour. Mrs V, a lone parent from Peru, had recently come to Britain with her daughters, Tania, and nine-year-old Miriam, after the girls' father had died from cancer in Peru. Since Mrs V was more comfortable speaking Spanish, an interpreter helped with all our meetings.

Abdul P

Eight-year-old Abdul P's father had died in a road traffic accident. Abdul was informed of his father's death whilst in hospital for treatment of the injuries that he had sustained in the same accident. He was refusing to eat and, formerly a jolly child with a sharp sense of humour, had not spoken for two days. Abdul's mother stayed with him in hospital. She described herself and her late husband as Moslem Asians from Africa.

Jamie M

Ten-year-old Jamie M had been diagnosed with leukaemia when he was 6. For the past four years, following a bone marrow transplant, he had been well. Shortly after his parents were told that his leukaemia had returned and that medical treatment could offer no more than palliative care, Jamie stopped speaking, and the medical team were concerned that he was depressed.

REFERENCES AND BIBLIOGRAPHY

Andersen, T. (1995). Reflecting processes: acts of informing and forming: you can borrow my eyes, but you must not take them away from me! In: S. Friedman (Ed.), *The Reflecting Team in Action. Collaborative Practice in Family Therapy*. New York: Guilford Press.

Anderson, H., & Goolishian, H. A. (1992). The Client is the Expert: a not-knowing approach to therapy. In: S. McNamee & K. J. Gergen (Eds.), *Therapy as Social Construction*. London: Sage.

Anderson, H., Goolishian, H. A., & Winderman, L. (1987). Problem determined systems: towards transformation in family therapy. *Journal of Strategic and Systemic Therapies*, 5 (4): 1–13.

Bateson, G. (1972). *Steps to an Ecology of Mind*. New York: Ballantine Books.

Bateson, G. (1979). *Mind and Nature*. London: Wildwood Press.

Black, D. (1994). Bereavement. In: A. Goldman (Ed.), *Care of the Dying Child*. Oxford: Oxford University Press.

Bluebond-Langner, M. (1978). *The Private Worlds of Dying Children*. Princeton, NJ: Princeton University Press.

Boscolo, L. (1989). "Falling in love with ideas". An interview with Luigi Boscolo by Max Cornwell. *Q.A.N.Z. Journal of Family Therapy*, 10 (2): 97–103.

Boscolo, L., Cecchin, G., Hoffman, L., & Penn, P. (1987). *Milan Systemic Family Therapy*. New York: Basic Books.

Bowlby, J. (1969). *Attachment and Loss, Vol. 1: Attachment*. London: Hogarth Press.

Bowlby, J. (1973). *Attachment and Loss, Vol. 2: Separation, Anxiety and Anger*. Harmondsworth: Penguin Books.

Bowlby, J. (1980). *Attachment and Loss, Vol. 3: Loss, Sadness and Depression*. New York: Basic Books.

Bowlby, J. (1989). *The Making and Breaking of Affectional Bonds*. London: Routledge.

Butler, R.N. (1968). The life review: an interpretation of reminiscence in the aged. In: B. N. Neugarten (Ed.), *Middle Age and Aging*. Chicago, IL: Chicago University Press.

Cecchin, G. (1987). Hypothesizing, circularity and neutrality revisited: an invitation to curiosity. *Family Process, 26*: 405–413.

Cecchin, G., Lane, G., & Ray, W. A. (1992). *Irreverence. A Strategy for Therapists' Survival*. London: Karnac Books.

Cecchin, G., Lane, G., & Ray, W. A. (1994). *The Cybernetics of Prejudices in the Practice of Psychotherapy*. London: Karnac Books.

Cronen, V. E., Johnson, K. M., & Lannaman, J. W. (1982). Paradoxes, doublebinds and reflexive loops: an alternative theoretical perspective. *Family Process, 20*: 91–112.

Cronen, V. E., & Lang, P. (1994). Language and action: Wittgenstein and Dewey in the practice of theory and consultation. *Human Systems, 5*: 5–45.

Cronen, V. E., & Pearce, W. B. (1985). Toward an explanation of how the Milan method works: an invitation to a systemic epistemology and the evolution of family systems. In: D. Campbell & R. Draper (Eds.), *Applications of Systemic Family Therapy*. London: Grune & Stratton.

Epston, D. (1992). Strange and novel ways of addressing guilt. In: D. Epston & M. White, *Experience, Contradiction, Narrative and Imagination. Selected Papers of Donald Epston and Michael White 1989–1991*. Adelaide: Dulwich Centre.

Epston, D., & White, M. (1990). Consulting your consultants: the documentation of alternative knowledges. In: D. Epson & M. White, *Experience, Contradiction, Narrative and Imagination. Selected Papers of Donald Epston and Michael White 1989–1991*. Adelaide: Dulwich Centre.

Freud, S. (1916–17). *Introductory Lectures on Psychoanalysis. Standard Edition, 15–16*. London: Hogarth Press.

Freud, S. (1917). Mourning and melancholia. *Standard Edition, 14*. London: Hogarth Press.

Furman, E. (1974). *A Child's Parent Dies: Studies in Childhood Bereavement*. New Haven, CT: Yale University Press.

Goldman, A. (1994). *Care of the Dying Child*. Oxford: Oxford University Press.

Goldman, A., & Christie, D. (1993). Children with cancer talking about their own death, with families. *Paediatric Haematology and Oncology, 10*: 223–231.

Hargreaves, R. (1978). *Mr Grumpy*. Los Angeles, CA: Price Stern Sloan.

Imber-Black, E. (1991). Rituals and the healing process. In: F. Walsh & M. McGoldrick (Eds.), *Living Beyond Loss. Death in the Family*. New York: W. W. Norton.

Judd, D. (1989). *Give Sorrow Words. Working with a Dying Child*. London: Free Association Books.

Kane, B. (1979). Children's conceptions of death. *Journal of Genetic Psychology, 134*: 141–153.

Kendrick, C., Culling, J., Oakhill, T., & Mott, M. (1987). Children's understanding of their illness and its treatment within a paediatric oncology unit. *Association of Child Psychology and Psychiatry, 8*: 2–5.

Kubler-Ross, E. (1970). *On Death and Dying*. New York: Macmillan.

Kubler-Ross, E. (1983). *On Children and Death*. New York: Macmillan.

Mendez, C. L., & Maturana, H. R. (1988). The bringing forth of pathology. *The Irish Journal of Psychology, 9* (1): 144–172.

Menzies, I. (1959). The functioning of social systems as a defence against anxiety. In: I. Menzies-Lyth, *Containing Anxiety in Institutions*. London: Free Association Books, 1988.

Middleton, D., & Edwards, D. (1990). Conversational remembering: a social psychological approach. In: D. Middleton & D. Edwards (Eds.), *Collective Remembering*. London: Sage.

Nagy, M. H. (1959). The child's view of death. In: H. Feifel (Ed.), *The Meaning of Death*. New York: McGraw-Hill.

Orbach, I., Gross, Y., Glaubman, H., & Berman, D. (1985). Children's perception of death in humans and animals as a function of age, anxiety and cognitive ability. *Journal of Child Psychology and Psychiatry, 26* (3): 453–463.

Palazzoli, M., Boscolo, L., Cecchin, G., & Prata, G. (1980). The problem of the referring person. *Journal of Marital Family Therapy, 6* (1), 3–9.

Parkes, C. M. (1972). *Bereavement: Studies of Grief in Adult Life*. New York: Pelican.

Pearce, W. B. (1994). *Interpersonal Communication: Making Social Worlds.* New York: Harper Collins College.

Piaget, J. (1958). *The Child's Construction of Reality.* London: Routledge & Kegan Paul.

Rothenberg, M. (1974). Problems posed for staff who care for the child. In: L. Burton (Ed.), *Care of the Child Facing Death.* London: Routledge and Kegan Paul.

Silverman, P. R., Nickman, S., & Worden, J. W. (1991). Detachment revisited: the child's reconstruction of a dead parent. *American Journal of Orthopsychiatry, 62:* 93–104.

Tomm, K. (1988). Interventive interviewing. Part III: Intending to ask lineal, circular, strategic, or reflexive questions? *Family Process, 27* (1): 1–15.

Watzlawick, P., Beavin, J., & Jackson, D. (1967). *Pragmatics of Human Communication: A Study of Interactional Patterns, Pathologies and Paradoxes.* New York: W.W. Norton.

White, M. (1989a). The externalizing of the problem and the re-authoring of lives and relationships. In: White, M. *Selected Papers.* Adelaide: Dulwich Centre Publications.

White, M. (1989b). Saying hullo again: the incorporation of the lost relationship in the resolution of grief. In: M. White, *Selected Papers.* Adelaide: Dulwich Centre Publications.

White, M. (1991). Deconstruction and therapy. In: D. Epston & M. White, *Experience, Contradiction, Narrative and Imagination. Selected Papers of David Epston and Michael White 1989–1991.* Adelaide: Dulwich Centre Publications.

White, M., & Epston, D. (1990). *Narrative Means to Therapeutic Ends.* New York: W. W. Norton.

Wittgenstein, L. (1953). *Philosophical Investigations.* Oxford: Basil Blackwell.

Worden, J. W. (1991). *Grief Counselling and Grief Therapy. A Handbook for the Mental Health Practitioner.* London: Routledge.

INDEX

abilities, valuing, 107–114
acceptance, 41
  vs. denial, 44
  of loss, as task of mourning, 42
  as stage of dying, 41, 128
adjusting, as task of mourning, 42
age:
  relevance of to beliefs about death,
    79
  rituals appropriate for, 84
ancestors, importance of, 31
Andersen, T., xxiv, 120
Anderson, H., xxv, 5, 63
anger, 50, 57
  in death or bereavement, 48
  emotion constructed as, 50
  helping family or client to express,
    41, 49
  negative connotations ascribed to
    in children's books, 50
  as phase of mourning, 42, 128
  as stage of dying, 41, 128
anxiety, about death, 58
  defence against, 13
  managing, xix
art, representation of death in, 31

bargaining, as stage of dying, 41,
  128
Bateson, G., xxiv, xxv, 18, 62, 72
Beavin, J., xxiv
behaviour:
  as communication, 22–23

  reorganized, as phase of
    mourning, 42
behavioural psychology, xviii
beliefs:
  about death, exploring with
    families, xxi
  observing (Exercise 3), 103–106
  use of as resource, 107–113
bereavement:
  pathological, 4–5, 11, 103, 104, 105
  denial as symptom of, 44
  diagnosis and treatment of, 104
  psychological theories and
    techniques for, xviii, xxi, 41
  work, conventional practices in,
    xix
  See also mourning
Berman, D., 128
Black, D., 44
Bluebond-Langner, M., 22, 26, 34, 37
books, children's, 131–136
  as source of death stories, 63
  using (Exercise 6), 117–118
Boscolo, L., xxii, xxiv, xxv, 5, 43
Bowlby, J., xviii, 41, 42, 128
Butler, R. N., 19

Cecchin, G., xxii, xxiv, xxv, 5, 14, 46
ceremonies, 79, 80, 83
  co-evolving, xxii
  mourning, 78
    for healing and celebration, 83
    preferred, 80